ONCE MY CHILD... NOW MY FRIEND

ALSO BY ELINOR LENZ

So You Want to Go Back to School (coauthor)
Effectiveness Training for Women (coauthor)

ELINOR LENZ

ONCE MY CHILD... NOW MY FRIEND

 **WARNER BOOKS**

A Warner Communications Company

Warner Books, Inc., 75 Rockefeller Plaza, New York, N. Y. 10019

 A Warner Communications Company

Distributed in the United States by Random House, Inc., and
in Canada by Random House of Canada, Ltd.
Printed in the United States of America
First Printing: May 1981
10 9 8 7 6 5 4 3 2 1

Book design by Helen Roberts

Grateful acknowledgment is made for permission to reprint copyrighted
material:

From "The Ballade of Lost Objects" in *Times Three* by Phyllis McGinley.
Copyright 1953 by Phyllis McGinley. Originally appeared in *The New Yorker*.
Reprinted by permission of Viking Penguin Inc. (New York) and Martin
Secker & Warburg (London).

From "The Last of October" by Ted Walker. Originally appeared in *The New
Yorker*. Reprinted by permission of Harold Ober Associates.

Library of Congress Cataloging in Publication Data

Lenz, Elinor.
   Once my child . . . now my friend.

   1. Parenthood—United States. 2. Parent and
child—United States. 3. Social role.
I. Title.
HQ755.8.L47   306.8'7   80-24983
ISBN 0-446-51224-9

To
Mollie, who showed me how to be
a daughter

Leo, who helped me become a parent

Stephanie and Lilli, who helped me
become an ex-parent

Robina, who many years ago taught me
what it means to be a friend

Acknowledgments

I am grateful to all those who shared
with me their experiences as parents
and ex-parents, children and ex-children.
I also want to thank Christine Conrad and
Mike Hamilburg, whose support and
enthusiasm nourished me throughout the
writing of the book.

Contents

PART I

On the Way to Ex-parenthood

Prince, I warn you, under the rose,
   Time is the thief you cannot banish.
These are my daughters, I suppose,
   But where in the world did the children vanish?
      —Phyllis McGinley, "Ballade of Lost Objects"

1
Once a Parent

An ex-parent is someone who has assisted in the transformation of a small helpless creature into a full-grown, unique human being, capable of independent thought and action. As the parent becomes an "ex," all links of dependency with the child are dissolved, and the remaining ties are those of friendship, sympathy, understanding, and acceptance of each other's individuality. When this relationship has been achieved, both parent and child have moved safely into the stage of ex-parenthood.

Moments of revelation come in as many disguises as blessings. For me there was a particular moment, a sudden flash of insight, which came cleverly disguised as a casual conversation with my thirty-year-old daughter. We were having tea in the living room of her North London home, where she lives with her actor-director husband and two small

3

daughters. My annual two-week visit was nearing an
end and our conversation for the past hour or so had
consisted mainly of shallow diggings into family
matters: an aunt's retirement, a cousin's divorce, a
diagnosis of cancer in an uncle-by-marriage.

I no longer recall exactly what prompted my
daughter's illuminating comment. It may have been
sparked by my repetition of the word "our"—including her in the nuclear foursome that was completed
by my husband and younger daughter, neither of
whom had been able to accompany me on this trip. In
any case, what she said was: "Of course, if I had to
choose between my family and your family, I would
quite naturally choose mine."

Yours and mine. I had never thought of it that
way. For me, her family had always been an extension of ours. We were root and stock: they an offshoot, implanted on foreign soil to be sure, but all
the same, a branch, joined firmly and forever to its
native source. But she was seeing two separate
plantings, not only growing in different soils but carrying within them the seeds of competition and conflict. I could not—still cannot—conjure up a situation
that would pit her and hers against me and mine.
When I look at her, my own young woman's face
looks back at me. The grayish-green eyes, the mouth
with its short pointed upper lip, the squared-off chin
are mine, and so are her quick, nervous gestures, her
compulsive enthusiasms, her moodiness and self-preoccupation. In so many ways, she is my persona,
clothed in younger flesh. And yet there she was, dis-
avowing this bond, as if by an act of psychosurgery
that severed us neatly from each other and left me
groping for some postoperative identity tailored to
fit our new relationship, whatever that might be.

Ex-mother. That would have to do for the time being. We were two women at different stages of the life cycle. We had some shared memories. Some of our deepest values made a good match, others clashed gratingly. No matter. From here on, whatever we were to be to each other would have to be improvised as we went along. I could make no further claims upon biology, nor could I draw upon the capital accumulation of past commitments and obligations. I would have to stand on my own, depend on my own resources. It was, for the moment, an unsettling prospect that left me feeling shaken and betrayed.

On the plane returning to California a scene from the past projected itself on the screen of my memory. I was lying on a bed in a hospital in New York, miscarrying my first child, or "fetus," as I tried to think of it, hemorrhaging profusely and waiting to be taken to the operating room to be curetted. On one side of my bed stood my mother, on the other my husband, two sturdy survivors who had carefully staked out their emotional territories in my life and were there exercising their proprietary rights.

"When you're ready," my mother said, "you'll come home with me. I'll take care of you."

My husband stared steadily at my mother across my inert body. "She's my wife," he said. "When she's ready, she comes home with me and *I* take care of her."

That could have been a moment of revelation for my mother. But I think it must have taken many such moments before she realized, if she ever did, that the parental bond is not forged of unbreakable steel. She came, after all, from a generation in which once a parent, always a parent.

Not long after my conversation with my daughter, I had a call from my friend Paula. It was on the day her divorce became final.

"I'm an ex-wife," she said. "I'm in limbo, somewhere between single and married. It's like having a leg amputated. I still feel George's presence and even, sometimes, the pain. But it's also a kind of relief." I knew exactly what she meant. She had clung to the marriage long after it deserved a decent burial, trying to beat life into the carcass with bribery, blackmail, and appeals to guilt and pity, because, as she said: "I'm forty-eight years old and I look it. My children don't need me anymore. They sound bored and impatient when I phone them. Funny, but now that it's settled, I don't mind so much about George. A husband can be replaced—and I've got my eye on a man in my condominium association—but you can't replace your children. I guess nothing hurts as much as feeling you've failed as a parent."

A woman I once fell into conversation with on a flight to New York said, "We were a lost generation, the women of the fifties who were brainwashed into believing that marriage and motherhood would last a lifetime." And their men, she might have added, who became candidates for ulcers and angina as they struggled single-handedly to pay the fees of parenthood: the orthodontists' bills, the skiing vacations, the college tuition and board—only to find that what this purchased was a daughter on drugs, a son announcing coolly at the dinner table, "I'm splitting. You represent everything I despise."

I think of Edna living in a one-room apartment in Los Angeles, her only son, Rick, divorced three times and jailed once on a drug possession charge, now living in San Francisco with his male lover.

Edna blames herself: "I had an affair when Rick was fourteen years old. Greg and I were still living together, but the marriage was coming apart. Rick was very close to his father. They had one of those camping-fishing-hunting relationships from which I, of course, was excluded, and when Rick found out about me, it changed him from an easygoing, agreeable boy into a moody, hostile little monster. I thought at the time it was just adolescence, but now I realize what happened to him. He was at the most sexually vulnerable time of his life—and he learned to distrust and despise women."

Edna lives more frugally than her salary as an accountant requires; whatever she can spare goes to her son—guilt money, a self-imposed tax that she will continue to pay for the rest of her life, unless she is able somehow to make the transition to ex-parenthood.

How Did We Get Here from There?

The path to postparenthood is as pitted and scarred as the surface of the moon, and much of it is strewn with the wreckage of mutual trust and aspirations. The parental mea culpa "where did I go wrong?" has become the unfunny joking question for the age. Our assumption that parents are all-powerful and therefore all-responsible for what their children become has created a climate in which guilt and recrimination are as inevitable as death and taxes. It is one of our most deeply held beliefs, a legacy of Freud, that the behavior of the parent toward the child—rejection, restriction, authoritarianism, or extreme permissiveness—can result in severe psychological disorders in later life, such as depression, schizophrenia, frigidity, homosexuality, criminal behavior.

Burdened with such an awesome responsibility and locked in the constricting embrace of the nuclear family, tensions and resentments build up that, left to fester, frustrate efforts to develop healthy relationships during adolescence and adulthood. When parent and child confront each other as adults, the silent accusations are like an insistent drumbeat behind the silences and the spoken words that serve as a smoke screen for the emotions.

FATHER: Why didn't you turn into the brilliant scientist I always wanted to be? I never had the opportunity, but you had it and you threw it away. So here you are, a laid-back drifter hopping from job to job with no purpose and no future.

SON: So I have to act the lead in your script in order to get your applause. Why didn't you help me write my own script?

MOTHER: Why don't you find a man you can marry and have children with? All my friends are grandmothers. When they tell me about their grandchildren, all I can talk about is your Siamese cat. So you're a lawyer, hooray. But shacking up with one man after another. When they've got what they want from you, they go their merry way. And where will you be when you're forty?

DAUGHTER: Your clock stopped thirty years ago and you don't even know it. You still think a woman's life is marriage and children. Nothing else counts. I've busted my guts trying to amount to something, and it means nothing to you. There's no way I can prove myself to you—except by getting a man to marry me and make me pregnant, something any moron can do.

The inner dialogue goes on, breaking occasionally to the surface, in emotional eruptions that leave a deposit of bitterness in their wake, a harsh lava difficult to dissolve. How, each wonders, could the people we once were, the feelings we once had for each other, turn into this? How did we get here from there?

The answer is often embedded in the distorted image of the parent and the grown child, in the fact that they are looking past each other at their interior visions instead of the flesh-and-blood people they really are. They are out of phase, moving through different cycles of the life span. The parent may be experiencing that contemporary angst, the midlife crisis, thrashing about in what feels like a stagnant and bottomless pool. A job that's dead-ending. A marriage going stale. Time slipping away and nothing to show for it.

The adult son or daughter is feeling another kind of panic. What am I going to do with my life? What if I never amount to anything, if nothing ever works out? There's nothing to fall back on, no one to take care of me anymore. I've got to make it all by myself.

Even their fear of failure is pointed in opposite directions. The adult child's concern is with the possibility of future failure, the parent's anxieties are centered on the failure that is lurking in the past. This failure syndrome among parents and children is in many ways peculiarly American. We are a society that places a high value on parenthood. Achieving success as a parent runs a close second to succeeding at earning a living. Though the baby boom may be over, parenthood continues to enjoy a high rating, and the national preoccupation with the raising of the young shows no signs of tapering off.

The desire to do a good job as parents has transformed what was once regarded as a natural function into a self-conscious, quasi-professional activity. Since affection and instinct are no longer regarded as sufficient for the complex and serious task of rearing a new generation, manuals and guides to parenting are studied assiduously, and the theories of various "experts" are consulted, compared, and debated by conscientious parents or parents-to-be. Workshops, seminars, and training programs for parents are thriving, and counselors concentrating on parent-child relationships are doing a brisk business. A training institute in southern California that specializes in teaching "communication skills" to parents employs thousands of trainers around the country; parents flock to these classes to learn how to listen to their children and how to talk to them without producing guilt or hostility.

But for all this activity, the parenting script is curiously foreshortened, like a story that breaks off in the middle. There are no Dr. Spocks, no workshops or seminars for "empty nest" parents, for men and women in their midyears whose children have grown to adulthood and are living lives of their own. This period of parenting has been treated with benign neglect, as if all the parent-child problems magically disappear as soon as the child becomes an adult, as if a relationship so basic and so complex can be turned off like a spigot at some specific moment in time.

Why this missing piece in the family portrait? It is certainly not an accidental omission but rather the logical consequence of the head-spinning changes that have been taking place in the parent-child relationship. Not too long ago the problem of parents and grown children barely existed for the simple reason that most people died by the time their children were grown. With the extension of the life span, many people are now living twice as long as their ancestors, a situation that has enlivened and complicated the human condition with scenarios like these:

- The ninety-three-year-old resident of a nursing home who wept at the death of his "child," aged seventy-two.

- The fifty-five-year-old grandmother returning to school as a college freshman, attending classes with her eighteen-year-old granddaughter.

- The couple in their seventies marrying, each for the third time, over the objections of their middle-aged children.

- The devoted wife, mother, and grandmother, who, widowed at sixty, suddenly turns into a swinger and embarks upon a series of affairs, including one with her ex-son-in-law.

Gerontologist Bernice Neugarten says that our society is becoming accustomed to the twenty-two-year-old mayor, the thirty-year-old college president, the thirty-five-year-old grandmother, the fifty-year-old retiree, the seventy-year-old student, and even the eighty-five-year-old mother who is caring for a sixty-five-year-old child.

Life changes like these come about through drastic alterations in attitudes, in the way we think and feel about each other. Parents and children one hundred or even fifty years ago would hardly recognize their present-day counterparts. In the not too distant past the parent-child relationship rested on the principle that the child was the parents' property. Soames Forsyte in the famous *Forsyte Saga* looks down at his newborn daughter in her cradle and says, "This is *mine.*" The family of our parents and grandparents was a tightly knit unit, a source of identification for all living generations. Parental, usually paternal, authority and power were accepted as a fact of life. And the elders' control did not weaken as the younger generation grew to adulthood; in fact, in higher-income families it was strengthened as the family wealth and prestige increased.

This extension of the parental role into the children's adult lives was found also among the hardworking majority of the population. In farm families, in which parents and children worked side by side, when the time came for the adult children to take over the day-to-day operations of the farm, the parents usually remained on the premises, often retaining legal ownership until their death. The close-knit nature of the family survived even the early years of urbanizing and industrializing, mainly because, in the pre-jet age, there was a low level of mobility. The New York apartment that was my childhood home housed three generations, and it was unthinkable for any of the grown children to settle more than a ten-minute subway ride away from Mama and Papa. Had I done my parenting at that time, it is unlikely that I would have had a daughter living across the ocean seven thousand miles away.

In an environment of such hothouse closeness, parents and children inevitably knew a great deal about each other. Secrets were difficult to keep. And there was not much scope for developing, on either side of the generational boundary, illusions or false expectations. We can estimate the distance we have traveled when we consider the recent Supreme Court ruling that a teen-age girl need not tell her parents that she is planning to have an abortion.

How did we get here from there? Those of us whose growing-up years were in the forties and fifties or earlier have been catapulted into a world we never made, in which the bulk of what we learned in our impressionable years has been tossed into the discard. Our adaptation mechanisms are badly overstrained and may need to be retooled or replaced. But that's only part of the story, the easy part. It's always comforting to blame the times for our troubles, to place the responsibility on external forces— fate or God's will or the position of the stars at the moment of our birth. The more difficult and more crucial part is the allocation and acceptance of personal responsibility. For parents, especially those with grown children, this has been a major source of conflict and confusion. Until we can bring some clarity to this cloudy area, there is little chance of our developing into successful ex-parents.

These years of our lives, the middle and later years, can be our most rewarding, most fulfilling, most creative period. Relieved of the burdens of parenthood, we are now free to discover our true identity, realize our personal potential, search out new friends, interests, sexual diversions. Everything is open to us, everything is possible. We can live longer, stay healthier, and remain on the job past the

formerly accepted legal limit. As our numbers increase—and the demographic projections are on our
side—we can expect to have more political power.
Books and articles and special magazines about us
are pouring off the presses. We have our own television programs. Colleges and universities, alarmed
by the declining enrollment of the young, are inviting us to continue our education. Advertising agen-
cies, sensing a market, are pausing in their relentless
pursuit of the Pepsi Generation to take note of our
need for dentures and laxatives.

The message is coming through loud and clear:
Youth is no longer the one and only time of wine and
roses. Now that the geometry of the life span has
been revised—from linear to cyclical—our salad
days are considered just a stage on the journey, and
as we travel the now predictable route (so we're
told), we'll find that each stage is as good as any other, with its own pleasures, tensions, traumas, and, in
Erik Erikson's term, its own special "task."

But if the promise of the mid and later years is
to be realized, if we are to enjoy to the fullest this
second blooming, we shall need to have a firm grasp
of where we are and who we are and how we can develop the identity of an ex-parent. And we'll have to
learn to avoid some of the booby traps along the
way. Two, in particular.

The Obsolete Role

Some years ago Philip Wylie wrote a book in
which he identified the source and origin of all our
disorders as the devouring, soul-destroying all-
American Mom. Taken up eagerly by the media, she

stood accused of, among other sins, emasculating her sons, inducing frigidity in her daughters and turning her mate into a cowed, ineffectual lump. In time she acquired ethnic trappings and, with an assist from Philip Roth, emerged full-blown as the Jewish Mother. What's more, you didn't have to be Jewish to be one, as the saying went. In fact, in "The Negro Family: The Case for National Action," Daniel Moynihan's famous study of the black family, there she was, presiding over her brood with iron fist in velvet glove.

The profile of this folk heroine, who has contributed so much to American lore, looks like this: She represents a kind of rock-ribbed authority within the family, and her faith in this institution is unswerving. That the family might ever decline—that kinship ties, as the sociologists put it, might loosen and be replaced by other forms of association—this is something she could never countenance.

Her rule rests essentially on two supports: food and guilt. Oblivious to calories or cholesterol, she cooks in prodigious quantities, and her familiar injunction to "eat, eat, my child" is unquestioningly obeyed, domestic peace having a higher priority than digestive comfort. She is fiercely loyal and protective toward her children, and when their behavior runs counter to her own plans for them, she can feign a terminal illness with thespian skill worthy of an Academy Award. Her children are her life—so she is fond of saying—and she has gladly, willingly sacrificed her own ambitions and her personal needs and interests to devote herself to their welfare. It is a devotion that includes unremitting attention to the minutest details of their physical and emotional lives and that continues undiminished after the children are grown, married, with families of their own—in fact, until death parts her from her appointed rounds and ministrations.

The Jewish Mother served us well and faithfully during a time when first- and second-generation Americans were struggling upward to find their place in the American Dream and needed strong backup support within the family. But that time is past. We are no longer a nation of immigrants, and our identification with family and Mom is, for better or worse, weakening. Elizabeth Hardwick puts it this way: "Society does not want women to lead a long life in the home. It is not prepared to support them and cannot give the old style true sanction. Children do not want their parents' lives to be given to them forever. Husbands cannot take the responsibilities for wives as an immutable duty ordained by nature."[1]

It is time to offer a requiem for the Jewish Mother—and for her partner, the overworked husband and father, locked into his role as Provider, surrendering his votes on the day-to-day rearing of the children to his formidable mate. Many of us in the postparenthood stage were weaned and nurtured on these role models and we cling to them for lack of something to put in their place. But in the real world we inhabit they are obsolete and they present us with difficult obstacles to overcome on the path to postparenthood.

Discarding outworn parental roles does not mean that mothering and fathering need be less loving, less caring than before. What it points to is a more balanced family unit, with relationships based

[1]Elizabeth Hardwick, "Domestic Manners," *Daedalus* (Winter 1978).

not on possessiveness and manipulation but on self-awareness and mutual respect. These are relationships that reflect the realities of contemporary life. With changing attitudes toward marriage and the rising divorce rate, parents and children are finding themselves in such situations as these: children with single parents or two sets of parents; parents with children who have live-in mates or a string of ex-mates, legal or otherwise; parents and children in relationships with others of the same sex, and any number of combinations, permutations, and variations on the theme. The implication of all this is fairly clear: People will be relating to each other more and more as individuals rather than on the basis of their biological ties. Blood may prove to be thinner than friendship. Some of us will, of course, mourn the passing of strong, enduring kinship bonds, but developing other ties and resources in their place can be a form of self-preservation—protection against that other familiar trap of the mid and later years, which catches us in the middle between two generations.

The Generational Sandwich

From a therapist's files, transcript of a taping during an initial consultation with a fifty-four-year-old woman:

"I sometimes think I'm living in a bad dream and that I'm never going to wake up. My parents are both in their eighties, both in poor health, and since they've been divorced for over thirty years, they're in separate nursing homes, about an hour's drive from each other. I'm their only child and they always expected that I would comfort and care for them in their old age. They phone me constantly, at home and at the office. I try to visit them evenings after work and, whenever I can, over the weekend. My mother accuses me of spending more time with my father than with her, my father complains that I spend more time with her than with him. I have a twenty-five-year-old son who's an actor and he gets into these depressions when he's not working, which is most of the time. My twenty-three-year-old daughter is going through an unhappy love affair and has attempted suicide; she's being treated by a psychiatrist. Recently, I began breaking out in hives and having migraine headaches. I'm divorced, and for the last year I've been seeing a man I met through my work, but I had to break it off. There isn't enough of me left over from all my family problems to be much good to any man."

This is an extreme case, but it contains elements that are very familiar to those of us who are at that time of our lives when we feel we are being pressed out of shape between the needs of our growing or grown children and those of our aging parents. In many cases, we have allowed ourselves to be caught in this pincers movement through a series of complex behaviors that erode our personal identity and blur the boundary lines marking off our individual selves from the people closest to us. We have become so interdependent that we have lost all semblance of independence. And learning what it means to be both independent and interdependent is what ex-parenthood is all about.

The biological act of having a child is not a passport to instant parenthood. It takes a long time to become a parent, in the full sense of the word, and becoming an ex-parent also does not happen overnight. There are no quick answers or easy formulas for the problems and dilemmas of parenting and exparenting. But there are avenues that lead to a better understanding of those problems and dilemmas, and, through this understanding, to a more competent way of dealing with them. This book is an exploration of those avenues, and in the following chapters, as you discover how others have worked their way through their parental relationships to exparenthood, as you share in the counsel of psychologists, therapists, and others who are closely involved with the problems of parents and children at all stages of their lives, there is an excellent chance that you, too, will be able to move more confidently and effectively along the path to postparenthood.

2
When Is a "Child" an Adult?

There is no word in the English language for the "child" who is no longer a child. The six-year-old is your child and so is the sixty-year-old. It's "my son" and "my daughter," but, in the plural, whatever their age, it's "my children." This omission in our vocabulary tells us much about how we have internalized the parent-child relationship. The ninety-three-year-old referred to in the previous chapter was weeping for the loss of his "child," and the fact that the "child" was in his seventies did not in any way lessen the father's grief or alter his parental image of a creature still incomplete, a life cut off prematurely.

As long as your parents are alive, you are their "child." You may be supporting them financially, caring for them physically, acting as their guide and mentor. No matter. Somewhere in the recesses of their consciousness, you are a fledgling whose flight from the nest was precipitous and whose attempts to fly are fraught with risk and error. I know a forty-eight-year-old woman with three grown sons whose morning conversations with her eighty-year-old mother leave her limp and sweaty from the sheer effort of clamping down on her rising anger. The daily maternal news bulletins go something like this:

"I saw this new cream in the drugstore, it's for smoothing out wrinkles, so I bought you a jar. You don't have to pay me, it's a present. You shouldn't have so many wrinkles at your age, you should take better care of your skin. I ran into your friend Emily yesterday. She hasn't a line in her face and she's a year older than you; I know because she was a year ahead of you in school."

All this, of course, is well meant, intended for the "child's" own good. It's the parents' duty, isn't it, to do their best for the children, regardless of their age? And, after all, it doesn't hurt any less to see a son mess up his life at thirty-five than at eighteen, and when a daughter sobs on your shoulder, though she has children of her own, you suffer for her as you did when she came home from her first-grade class with tears streaming down her cheeks. Is there a time, any time, when you can put those parental feelings aside and leave your children to stumble along as best they can, even though you are certain they're heading for disaster?

When does a child become an adult? Where is the timetable or calendar we can consult to locate this critical moment?

When my memory wanders back through the past, it takes me into hazy regions marked "childhood"; "adolescence"; "youth"; "middle age" ... But the boundaries are blurred; I can find no signposts stating "Childhood Ends Here"; "You Are Now Entering Adolescence"; "Proceed with Caution." When did my childhood end? Was it when I started menstruating? In that unenlightened time, I wasn't sure what was happening to me, and my mother's embarrassed instructions that from now on I was not to let boys touch me left me puzzled. I didn't know any boys except my junior high school classmates and they had so far shown little inclination to talk to me, let alone touch me.

At the age of thirteen, Jewish boys at their bar mitzvahs proclaim: Today I am a man. But the "man" has many years to go before he can vote, drive a car, take out a bank loan, marry, or assume any of the customary responsibilities of an adult. When does the boy become a man, the girl a woman? Is it the first sex experience that takes us over the border into adulthood? This rite of passage has been a popular motif in folk tales and romantic fiction: the sleeping princess, in the role of the virgin, awakened into womanhood by the first act of sexual intercourse; or the obligatory initiation at the brothel for the young male, accompanied occasionally by Father, whose paternal duties included this means of ushering his son into manhood.

Sexual initiation might be a convenient way of marking out the maturing process, except that it doesn't mesh with reality. The celibate priest, the fifty-year-old virgin—are they children, adolescents, adults? What about the ten-year-old girl who has been raped, the twelve-year-old who is bearing a child? Should they be treated as adults, with all that this implies, legally, socially, psychologically? There is plenty of evidence that children are capable of engaging in most forms of adult sexual activity, and that it is social inhibitions that keep them from doing so openly and in larger numbers. But the sexually experienced child is, all the same, regarded as a child, and the sexually inexperienced adult as an adult, however we perceive these states of being.

There are some clues to be found in biology, in the physical changes that mark off one age from another. Adolescence is identified mainly by the spurt in growth and the development of the reproductive organs. Then from puberty to late middle age, the physiological changes are slower and subtler. We are in the time of ripening, of middle age, which, with today's advanced health care and cosmetics, can be extended far beyond the limits of earlier eras.

"How do you know you're forty?" Judith Viorst asks, for "aren't we, as the kids are, into yoga and Hermann Hesse, films and pollution and Vitamin C? Aren't we, in contrast to our parents twenty-five years ago, a thousand times more youthful and sexy and free?"[1]

Well, yes ... And so we have the parent as sexual competitor—in the person of thirty-eight-year-old Tess, joining the parties of her twenty-year-old daughter, Barbara. "I enjoy it," she says. "The music, the dancing, sharing a joint with the kids ... and when I'm in the mood, I get a kick out of turning on Barbara's boyfriends. Just to prove I can do it."

Barbara's reaction? A shrug and a toss of her long streaky-blonde hair. "My mother embarrasses me sometimes. She's always on the make. But she's got this need, you know, for guys to be panting after

[1]Judith Viorst, "How Do You Know You're Forty?" *New York Times Magazine* (February 6, 1977).

her. It's the only way she knows she really exists."

Still, time is the thief you cannot banish. Despite the Vitamin C and the plastic surgery and the hair transplants there is the relentless advance of the menopause, the weakening vision, the loss of vigor and resilience.

So there are some biological signposts. But how useful are they in defining our psychological age? Where in the age spectrum should we place Alice, forty-two years old by the calendar, occupation bank teller, who falls asleep with the aid of tranquilizers and Gothic novels? In her fevered dreams, she is running barefoot across a desolate heath, pursued by Roderick Granville, Squire Granville's impetuous son and heir, whose dark secret is known to her and her alone....

Alice had a brief disastrous marriage in her early twenties and is afraid to try again. She is also afraid of flying, riding in elevators, crowds, strangers, salesclerks, loud noises, hospitals, hearses, and anything suggestive of illness or death. The psychologist whom Alice visits now and then describes her as "a child in an adult body, a little middle-aged girl."

What it comes down to is: Our biological clocks are unreliable—unless they are synchronized with our psychological and cultural clocks. Becoming an adult involves not only who you are as the sum total of your genetic inheritance and life experience, but what kind of world you're living in. Custom, religion, education all play a part in defining the boundaries between childhood, adulthood, and old age. It's a much more complicated business than most of us realize, recognizing when our "child" has left childhood behind and become an adult.

The Prolonged Adolescence

To further complicate the problem, we now have a system for postponing adulthood indefinitely. We call the system "education," and we've been entrusting our children to it over the years for longer and longer periods of time. A hundred years ago less than 5 percent of those in the high school age group were in school; all the others were out of the system and at work. Today, at least 90 percent finish high school, and of these more than 25 percent go on to college. But that's only the beginning.

It is possible today to parlay a college diploma into an indefinite stay at the university. The system cooperates with student loans, scholarships, fellowships, M.A.'s, Ph.D.'s, postdoctoral work, post-postdoctoral work, teaching assistantships, research assistantships—all of the above, and more, for those who are willing to apply a little imagination and resourcefulness.

James Coleman says: "As the labor of children has become unnecessary to society, school has been extended for them. With every decade, the length of schooling has increased, until a thoughtful person must ask whether society can conceive of no other way for youth to come into adulthood."[2]

The advantages of staying on in school became obvious during the sixties when enrollment in college served as one way to stay out of Vietnam. And today schools are serving another purpose for which they were never intended—as "warehouses" for the

[2]James Coleman, *Youth: Transition to Adulthood* (Chicago: University of Chicago Press, 1974).

young, keeping them off the labor market at a time of high unemployment. If the prospects of finding a job out there look dim, why not stay on another year or two or three, pick up another M.A. or maybe a law degree?

Meanwhile your Janey or Ronnie is approaching the midtwenties, or late twenties, or—is it possible?—edging past thirty, and of course, living a free and independent life: nice apartment convenient to campus, a succession of sex partners or maybe just one, earning a bit now and then from a stint of research or teaching. You're impressed with all the education this child of yours is stashing away and you help out financially as needed—mostly tuition fees not covered by the loans and scholarships, car maintenance because that's a necessity, and the annual vacation in Europe because Janey/Ronnie desperately needs a break after a tough year of classes and exams.

Sometimes you wonder whether Janey/Ronnie's education will ever be completed—you even joke about it with friends whose forty-year-old son has been working on his dissertation for the past five years—but after all, you're a hip and sensitive parent, you're tuned in to the Zeitgeist, you know where it's at. It takes the young a long time these days to "find themselves" in this tough and complex world. They need more preparation than you did; there are more options to sort out.

While they're sorting out the options, you're feeling that familiar tug at the umbilicus, and it's not entirely unpleasant. As long as Janey/Ronnie continue serving an apprenticeship, the future is open-ended and you still have a place in it, a hand in shaping the course of events, because without the financial aid you so freely and lovingly provide, Janey/Ronnie's school days would come to a sudden end. And then what? Then you would have to face something you may not be ready for—the test of your grown-up child's capacity for independence, for complete self-management, with all that this implies for your relationship. In other words, the future will be now, the fruition on which you have staked so much will be here, the plans and visions that have centered on this life that you have created and nurtured will come due, like promissory notes that must be paid in the hard currency of present-day reality.

There are, of course, other ways for today's young to put off becoming adults aside from staying in school. Turning off and dropping out are available in various sizes, shapes, and camouflages—from dropping acid to avoiding commitments. It may even be that extending the pre-adult years is a form of adjustment, a balancing out of the lengthening of the life span. The thirty-year-old who says "I don't know what I want to be when I grow up" isn't necessarily trying to be funny. He or she is simply recognizing that there is a long stretch of time ahead for being one thing or another—and it's not something to rush into.

What Adults Are Made of: A Parental Checklist

Though the concept of adulthood appears to be elusive and shifting, there is a growing body of research that may help us get a handle on it. Erik Erikson calls the adult stage "maturity," and as in the other seven stages of his scheme there is a tension specific to this period of development—in this case, between generativity, to use Erikson's term, and self-absorption. We generate, most commonly, by becoming parents, creators and custodians of the next generation. But is Erikson saying that becoming a parent automatically admits us to membership in the Association of Mature Adults? Not at all. The entrance requirement is nothing less than "maintenance of the world," by which Erikson means taking an active part in the life around us, even, where necessary, making changes in society's mores and institutions. But it's not a clear-cut choice between involvement and narcissism. The world is full of self-absorbed types who involve themselves in public activities for purely self-serving reasons. In fact, most of us are a mix of self-extension and narcissism, with one or the other taking over at various times in our lives as we respond to differing stimuli.

Among psychologists and family counselors the consensus is that the identifying marks of an adult should include:

Being aware of oneself as a unique and separate person, a self with whom one feels comfortable and on good terms, by a process that Jung calls "individuation."

Having the capability for effective management of one's own affairs. Being able to make one's way in an increasingly complex world without relying on the support or direction of others.

Taking responsibility for one's own actions.

Being open to the world and constantly striving to learn.

Making full use of one's personal resources.

Being capable of loving and making commitments to those one loves.

Recognizing that in addition to being a unique individual, one is also a member of a family and community.

How many of us, parent or child, could honestly lay claim to all of these attributes? But a score of 100 percent is not required in order to pass a test. If you can see in your grown children the lines of development suggested by the checklist, it is reasonable to assume that they are ready to be treated as adults.

The Critical Rite of Passage

Most parents want their children to become independent. We look forward to the time when they will be on their own, but the anticipation is tinged with dread. When the children go, we wonder anxiously, what will be left of us and of the family structure we have been so patiently building all these years and that we secretly believed, despite all rationality, would last forever?

Leaving home is a critical rite of passage for the parent as well as the child. Both are confronted by the supreme testing of the relationship: Can it survive the physical act of separation?

"You risk it," says a father of three, whose youngest, an eighteen-year-old daughter, had moved into her own apartment a month before. "You have no choice. I encouraged my daughter to leave, practically pushed her out, though I knew I was taking a chance. I wasn't sure she was ready for it, but it had to be done. She needed the psychological space which we as her parents couldn't give her—and we

needed to be relieved of the constant irritation of our
day-to-day contacts.

"We have some bad moments, I can tell you.
There've been a couple of rapes and burglaries in her
neighborhood. I think of her driving into that dark
garage in the evenings, and it's all I can do to keep
from going over there and dragging her back."

Family counselors believe that the first few
months after the child leaves are crucial to the future of the relationship. It's a sensitive, highly
charged period, this early stage of staking out a
fragile claim to independence. Any suspected challenge to the claim is very likely to meet with fierce
resistance. "I made a mistake with Ginny," said my
friend Paula. "A few weeks after she moved into her
apartment she went off for the weekend and left her
key with me so I could feed her cat. It was my first
visit to the apartment since she'd moved in—and you
wouldn't believe the mess—the stench of cat urine,
the garbage, the filth all over. You'd think she was
raised in a pigsty. I mean, I may not be Mrs. Clean,
but I've always taken pride in my housekeeping.
Well, I got to work, scrubbed and polished and vac-
uumed; went out and bought curtains for the windows and a new throw rug. I thought what a nice
surprise this will be for her. I pictured us having a
cup of coffee and chatting as we used to and she'd
tell me what a great job I'd done and how grateful
she was, and we'd be close again, the way it was
when she was growing up. And you know what? She
was furious. Said she didn't want me interfering, she
could take care of her own place, and would I please
get off her back? Well, I guess I should have known
better. But hell, after a lifetime of doing for your

kids, how are you supposed to suddenly switch it off? I mean, what was I supposed to do with the rest of my life?"

The "Empty Nest" Blues

It's not exactly news that the classic symptoms of postparenthood—loneliness and depression—are most severe for the woman who, like Paula, has been a full-time wife and mother. My generation of women, raising our families in the postwar pre-women's lib years, were early victims of what has come to be known as "the empty-nest syndrome." With Dr. Freud and Dr. Spock as our gurus, we were pushovers for the notion that we represented some sort of Primal Mother, with the power to make of our children a super-species. Who at that time could resist such a role and such a challenge? We applied ourselves with demonic zeal, placing our young firmly at the center of our personal universe, never doubting that, as creator of Super-kid, our rewards would be substantial and everlasting.

No wonder we felt we'd been had when we discovered that the rewards were empty, echoing rooms and a sense of being surplus property. Some of us went back to school or found a job or a lover or both. We coped, although there were those for whom the coping came out of a bottle. There was Roberta—Radcliffe, summa cum laude, with her fine-tuned intelligence and her Katharine Hepburn bone structure. The police picked her up one day wandering dazedly through the streets of Stamford, Connecticut. They phoned her husband, who had just moved into an apartment in New York with his secretary, and he drove out and took Roberta home. Later, over coffee with the smell of stale whiskey still in the air, they talked.

"Do you want me to come back? I'll come back," he said, adding quickly, "until you're on your feet again."

She shook her head, murmuring blurrily, "I miss Tom and Cindy."

"I'll phone them. They can be here by tomorrow. They can afford to skip a few days of school. Won't hurt them a bit. And they'll be good for you."

"No," she said, "I don't want them as they are now. I want them as they were—when they were little and I took care of them and they needed me."

Now, researchers tell us, there is another victim of the "empty nest"—the postparental father. As women go off to new interests and careers when their last child leaves, fathers are becoming more involved with their children. As a result, according to sociologist Robert Lewis, "The number of dispirited postparental fathers could be multiplying at the same time it appears that fewer mothers are experiencing crises with the launching of their children."[3]

A postparental father, sensitively described in a short story by Ted Walker, broods as he works in his garden: "Since my children had left home (both of them the previous summer), I'd spent a good deal of time doing jobs in the garden I'd neglected from year to year. I hadn't been able to contain my anger and bewilderment in the house. Why had they gone away

<hr>

[3]Alicia Fortinberry, "Father's Increasing Empty Nest Blues," *Psychology Today* (October 1979).

so abruptly? Why should two intelligent and well-loved young people desert their home for a commune? It made no sense to me."[4]

So now it's just as likely to be Dad who says, when eighteen-year-old Patty or Donald suggests getting a job and an apartment, "What's your hurry? Stay in school a few more years. There's plenty of time for working and paying the rent."

The Surrogate Husband

Leaving home takes place on two levels—the physical and the psychological—and the two may be far apart in time or the psychological departure may never take place. I came across one woman who said, "I know exactly when I became an adult. It was when I told my father to get out of my house. And by then I was a married woman with two teen-age sons."

This woman is in her mid-fifties, sleek, pant-suited, on the surface indistinguishable from those women whose natural habitat is Saks Fifth Avenue or I. Magnin. But only on the surface. There was a time, during the nesting and breeding years, when as the wife of a successful businessman her days were spent lunching and shopping. Now, working her way back from a two-year trauma of widowhood during which, as she says, "I woke up and fell asleep with the thought of a suicide," she is managing a Madison Avenue art gallery and learning to live alone without dissolving in tears and bourbon.

[4]Ted Walker, "The Last of October," *New Yorker* magazine (October 22, 1979).

She can talk about it calmly now.

"My father was an English professor and there was never much money, but I don't remember feeling deprived. I remember my mother as a nervous little appendage to my father; I used to wonder why my brilliant, forceful father married her. I thought God was made in my father's image. My father called me his little princess and it pleased me that he so obviously preferred me to my older sister. We lived in Brooklyn, not far from the museum, and my father used to take me there and to concerts and the theater, and in the evenings we read poetry to each other. My father was a strict disciplinarian and our family life was quiet and orderly.

"When my mother died, I was a senior in high school, and my sister married and moved to Chicago. I had planned to go to college and major in art history—the visits to the museum had taken effect—but instead I stayed home and kept house for my father. I met Michael, my husband, through a friend. I'd never known anyone like him before—he was wild and sexy and ambitious. His family was a mix of Irish and Italian—a noisy, scrapping, affectionate bunch—I don't think any of them ever heard of T. S. Eliot. I was bowled over by the contrast with our home environment.

"When Michael and I were married, we rented an apartment in Queens and Michael landed a public relations job in Manhattan. My father was retired by then and had plenty of time on his hands, and we went on pretty much as before—going to concerts and museums together and reading poetry—and I never made a decision without consulting him. Michael used to kid me about it, said my father was his toughest competition. My husband and my father didn't have much to talk about. Michael didn't care for art or poetry. Football and bowling were more in his line, but most of his energies went into his work—he was building up his own public relations business and doing very well. My father called Michael a huckster, which was probably true.

"The children were born eighteen months apart, and by that time I was too busy to go to concerts and museums. Michael's business was growing by leaps and bounds, and we bought a house in Great Neck and began entertaining on a lavish scale—mostly Michael's clients.

"My father made it clear he disapproved of the way we were living. He said things like—we were leading empty, sterile lives; our children were growing up in an intellectually impoverished environment. He said Michael was a Babbitt. Things like that.

"Of course I realized Michael was no intellectual, I accepted that, but I also knew he was a loving husband, a terrific father to our two boys, and an all-round good human being. I wanted my father to approve of my life and my family; I wanted it desperately. But I was also beginning to be aware of his uptightness, the rigid standards by which he measured the rest of the world. I had made this narrow, selfish man into my surrogate husband, and one day, I knew, there would have to be a 'divorce.'

"It happened one Sunday morning when he stopped in as I was clearing away the breakfast dishes; Michael and the boys were still asleep. We'd had one of our parties the evening before, and the place was a shambles: empty whiskey glasses, filled ashtrays, you can imagine. He looked around with an expression of disgust on his face. He said he thought he'd take the boys to the museum—there was a show of American Indian art they might enjoy. I told him the boys were planning to go to a football game with their father. I guess that did it. He launched into a tirade, attacking Michael, me, our way of life, our friends, our values. That was when I told him to leave my house and not come back until he was ready to apologize.

"He stood there, staring at me. I had never before spoken to him like that. He was in shock, and after a moment that seemed like a year he turned and walked out.

"The next time we met it was almost two years later—at Michael's funeral. He took me in his arms and held me—and we've been all right since then. We're growing into another relationship—I think we're finally becoming friends."

We may have found the missing word for the grown-up "child" who is no longer a child. The word is "friend," and it is the key to ex-parenthood. How do we become our children's friend? We can begin by working our way out of the confusions, misunderstandings, and unresolved conflicts that clog the circuits of communication between parents and their adult children.

3
Disconnecting: Phasing Out the Parent

How are you supposed to suddenly switch it off? Paula's plea perfectly expresses the frustration and bewilderment of parents at that moment of revelation when they discover that the behavior patterns they have developed over the years are no longer usable. The good-night kiss, the little fun gifts for special or no occasions, the bedside vigils, the shoulder to lean on, the advice freely sought and given, the achievements celebrated, the pangs of disappointment eased—all this is to be canceled without notice? All those invisible connections binding us together—is it possible to cut through them in one swift slash without doing damage to so much that is precious and irreplaceable?

Planned Ex-Parenthood

The sudden switch-off is no more likely to produce a healthy postparental relationship than the stubborn clinging to outworn behaviors. Between these extremes is a workable approach—the gradual disengagement, the phasing out of the role of parent while phasing in the role of ex-parent/friend. Slowly, but surely, we prepare for what lies ahead of us. We anticipate and plan for the predictable changes that will occur in our children's lives and ours, so that when they happen we are not knocked off our emotional balance.

Planning for parenthood is becoming the norm. For many people today the birth of a child is the result of a conscious decision, a matter of choice rather than an accident. But planning for ex-parenthood is still a rarity. Most of us bumble along from day to day as our children grow and go through changes and crises, expecting that somehow things will work themselves out. And when things turn out badly we agonize over what we could have done, how it could have been different.

In our effort to prop up the crumbling edifice of parenthood we resort to manipulative strategies:

Bribery: "I might be able to manage that ski outfit you've been hankering for if you——"

Appeal to guilt: "And the doctor said it's all this stress I've been under ever since you——"

Threat: "As long as you're living under my roof, you'll——"

Shaming: "I should think you'd be more considerate——"

Power play: "You'll never see another cent from me as long as you——"

Appeal from authority: "I've lived longer than you. I know better, take it from me——"

Unfavorable comparison: "I don't understand why you can't hold on to a job and the Elmans' son, who doesn't even have a college degree, is a sales manager, and last year, his mother tells me, he made, with salary and bonus——"

Dire prediction: "If you go on this way, you know how you're going to end up? Well, let me tell you——"

Invoking the dead: "It's a good thing your father/mother is no longer alive, because if he/she knew that you——"

But somehow these ploys only seem to hasten the collapse.

Why do we keep falling into these self-made traps? How is it that we tend to develop a sense of competence and control in our midyears in every area of our lives except the one that for most of us is the most important—parenthood? In this area the self-doubts and uncertainties seem to multiply as our children move into adulthood. Why does this happen?

As we delve into these puzzles and contradictions we begin to perceive that somewhere at the heart of the dilemma is a fundamental confusion about the parental relationship and the roles we assume within it.

The Three Connections

From the intricate network of connections that grow out of our commitments to each other we can identify three basic two-person relationships that provide the structure for human existence. All of our personal relationships are variants of these three:

1. Parent-child. Bond: biological or legal, as in the case of adoption or stepparenthood.
2. Lovers (all sexual unions, in or out of mar-

riage). Bond: sexual; also legal, as in marriage.
3. Friends. Bond: mutual interest.

What we have here is a trio of pairings, each with its own dynamics, and its own emotional chemistry. In the normal course of our development these relationships assume varying positions in our lives, taking shape as a life cycle of connections:

Early childhood. Parents are the powerful authority figures. Within the family structure created by the parents the helpless, dependent child seeks to grow toward independence and self-realization. In nuclear families the parents are the sole satisfiers of the small child's physical and emotional needs.

Adolescence. Friends now move into a leading position, providing intimacy, companionship, a sharing of interests and confidences, mutual validation of experience. With the weakening authority of family, school, and church, peers have become the prime influencers.

Early adulthood. Sexual relationships take first place as we strive toward intimacy, the emotional and physical union with another. Primary forces and emotions at this time are: sexual desire; love; jealousy; possessiveness; the need to establish one's sexual identity.

Mid-adulthood. The parent-child relationship again assumes the leading position, as the former child becomes the parent and is now the authority figure, the nurturer, the source of love, warmth, and support.

Late adulthood. During this postparental period the support system formerly provided by a growing family now rests upon friendships. Sexual relationships may also take on new importance, particularly when there is a divorce or the death of a spouse.

Old age.   Grandparenthood fulfills the need for continuity. Friendships provide links with the past and, as in adolescence, a sense of belonging to a community of peers. A parent-child role reversal may take place, with the mid-adult child becoming the parent of the parent.

As these relationships shift and fluctuate, they often become entangled with one another, and this is where the trouble starts. The attitudes and behaviors of one relationship are not easily transplanted to the other. Protection, nurturing, economic support, and an unequal balance of power form a pattern that is built into the parent-child relationship during the child's pre-adult years. Later, when the child becomes an adult, this early pattern may continue to exercise a strong hold on the adult child, emerging through all subsequent relationships either as a faithful simulation or a leap to the opposite extreme. For example, the girl who has always submitted to her authoritarian father will probably, when she is grown, be attracted either to macho "take charge" males or to the yielding submissive type who lets her take the lead. She may wonder why her relations with men are so unsatisfactory, never realizing that she is following the parent-child design, which doesn't work in sexual pairings any more than it does in friendships. The woman's movement is, in essence, a drive to free women from the patriarchal, or parental, bond that places them, vis-à-vis men, in the relation of a child to a parent. Friendship, on the other hand, is by definition "an attachment arising out of mutual esteem and good will"—or, to put it another way, a relationship between equals.

The transition from parent to friend occurs through a gradual process of inner change as we grow out of one set of attitudes and behaviors into another. It's not a surgical act—a cutting of the ties that leaves raw edges and a lasting residue of pain. We have to weave the ties into a new pattern that matches our new relationship.

"Divorce" for Parents and Children?

But suppose there are deep-seated conflicts between parent and child, conflicts that are rooted in the past and have grown to such proportions that there is no possibility of establishing amicable relationships between the antagonists? What about parents who really dislike their children—and vice versa—and prefer to break off all ties as soon as possible? Doesn't this type of situation call for some equivalent of marital divorce, which would separate parents and children, dissolving all legal and emotional bonds?

There are certainly instances in which the hostility and even raging anger between parent and adult child have reached such levels of intensity that only years of therapy could bring about any sort of reconciliation, and even therapy may not be able to do it. In these cases a complete break may be the only available solution. The idea of a parent-child "divorce" is very recent and grows out of contemporary concerns with the rights of individuals regardless of age, race, or gender. In Sweden, a child-divorce law has been proposed that would permit children to remain with foster parents, if they so wished, in the face of demands from the natural parents that their child be returned.

But these are atypical situations. For most of us the idea of a "divorce" from our children, whether they are biological or adopted, is unthinkable. Whatever our differences, whatever pain and disappointment are involved in the relationship, we have a mutual investment of emotion and experience that makes it difficult, if not impossible, for us to walk away from each other without a backward look.

As ex-parents, we are somewhat like those ex-wives and ex-husbands who become good friends after their marriage is dissolved. "We outgrew our marriage," the male half of one of these former couples recently remarked at a postdivorce seminar both were attending, "but we still have much to give each other; we have many interests and friends in common. Now that we're not forced to live together as husband and wife, we're freeing ourselves from the tensions of our marriage and we're becoming good friends." The former wife added, "We used to constrict each other—all that jealousy and possessiveness. Now we find we're stretching each other."

In becoming ex-parents and ex-children we can also stretch each other as we rid ourselves of the tensions and constraints, the labels and stereotypes that our roles have imposed upon us. We accomplish this not through "divorce" but through a revitalizing process of disconnection and reconnection.

In the Beginning

Phasing out of parenthood begins during our children's infancy as they learn to dress themselves, feed themselves, go to the toilet unassisted, and put themselves to bed. At this stage the separation of the child from the nurturing parent, who is usually the mother, happens with the parents' enthusiastic cooperation. How could we not be warmed by the sight of our children taking their first steps, uttering their first words, feeding themselves, and, in innumerable other ways, demonstrating their capacity for self-care?

But as they grow toward adulthood we become less enthusiastic about our children's efforts to go their own way, particularly when these efforts take them in directions that we find incomprehensible and alien. As our children begin to move out of the home and into the world beyond, we fall into a familiar parental negativism—a habit of naysaying to many of their initiatives, their urges to explore and experiment. Saying no to children who are not yet capable of self-care is, of course, a necessary way of expressing the desire to protect them from danger. But when this response develops into something like a knee-jerk reaction applied indiscriminately, it becomes a form of control. This type of behavior, known in psychology as Gregory Bateson's "double bind" theory, has exactly what it takes to produce schizoid symptoms: First the parents encourage the child's independence, then react negatively when the child asserts independence.

The Pygmalion Impulse

In subtle and unsubtle ways we impose inhibitions upon our children during their growing years. We settle their disputes for them, supervise their choice of friends, and stifle their curiosity and sense of adventure when these threaten to clash with our values and life style. In our attempt to model our children in our own image, knowingly or unknowingly we overlook their individual drives and potentialities and instead treat them as plastic human material, to be shaped following the social, ethnic, religious, and other requirements of the family. Like Pygmalion, who fell in love with the statue he created, we try to mold our children into adults whom we can love—who will be as much like us as possible or, rather, as we would like to be.

But this Pygmalion impulse in parents has its natural limits. Potent as our influence may be, the child is not putty in our hands. "Although nothing would induce me to underestimate the well-nigh incalculable importance of parental influence," Jung has said, "the decisive factor must be looked for in the disposition of the child." Ascribe it to the DNA code or the life force or whatever religious explanation you prefer, there is within every human being a core of individuality that is the basic material of the personality. There is much that parents can do with this material, but that stubborn core, the quintessential "I" remains intact, even when it must go underground to preserve itself.

Then, too, parents are only one of the many forces that work upon the child. In the life cycle of connections, we've seen that peers take a prominent position during the adolescent years. A midwestern father of my acquaintance complains: "All you've got with your kids is eight or nine years; then the peer group takes over." And the more control the parents have been exerting over the child all along, the greater will be the child's susceptibility to peer pressure.

The mass media are another strong shaping force, and television, the mechanical baby sitter, is conceded to be a formidable socializing agent, although the full extent of its effect upon growing minds is still being debated and explored by researchers.

And yet parents continue to believe that they have the godlike power to shape their children according to their private vision. "They are not merely trying to make the child well-behaved," observes Philip Slater in *The Pursuit of Loneliness;* "for them, personality is not a given, but something the parent can mold." They harbor the conviction that they are qualified and competent to steer their sons and daughters toward the appropriate occupation (the "my-son-the-doctor" syndrome), not to mention the most satisfactory marriage and way of life. In maintaining these delusions, they are aided by selective vision and hearing—the ability to filter out any information that cannot accommodate their parental expectations.

The Power of Expectations

Reality is no match for a parent with an ironclad set of expectations. From the moment of the child's birth the parent is making plans, conjuring up visions. The child will be the fulfiller of parental hopes and dreams and thwarted ambitions. Through the child a parent is born again, can correct past mistakes, and make up for past hurts and disappointments.

There is the father who grew up in an impoverished broken home and is determined to make his family financially secure and personally stable. In his effort to achieve security he develops tunnel vision and loses sight of his children's other needs in the world beyond the confines of home. He doesn't see that the children have their own insecurities, which are no less serious for them than his childhood difficulties were for him.

There is the mother whose own mother had been stern and unyielding and who was always the loser in the competition with her sister for the meager maternal rations of affection and attention. With her own children she is loving and easygoing, but there is one unbreakable rule: no competition. Everyone cooperates, all the time. Any show of selfishness or one-upmanship is firmly discouraged. No child is allowed to win an argument or benefit from a selfish or competitive act. The mother's distorted lens prevents her from seeing that she is depriving her children of outlets for their aggressive impulses, which must be forced underground, at the risk of breaking out later in more damaging forms.[1]

All through their growing up years children are receiving messages that, decoded, are an expression of parental expectations. The expectations change from one generation to the next. My parents, who

[1]Hess and Handel study of Chicago families, in Robert W. White, *The Enterprise of Living: Growth and Organization in Living*, 2nd ed. (New York: Holt, Rinehart and Winston, 1976).

were the children of immigrants, wanted us to be educated, respected, professional people. My mother, who left school at the age of twelve to work ten hours a day at a sewing machine, had one consuming idea—that my brothers and I were to be college graduates. When I dropped out of Hunter College during a time of desperate unhappiness, my mother took to her bed with a "heart condition." She lay in the darkened room, limp and pale, moaning now and then, refusing food: "I'm too weak to eat. But you shouldn't worry about me. If God wants me to go, I'm ready. Only—I had hoped that I could live to see my children graduate from college." I gave up a chance at a job as a reporter on *The New York Times*, returned to college, and she miraculously recovered.

We, the parents of the forties and fifties, borne along on the tidal wave of postwar affluence, had a different set of expectations for our young. We wanted them to be cultured, creative, and, if we came of immigrant stock, to complete the process of merging into the American mainstream. As we projected our fantasies onto our sons and daughters, they became the instruments by which our own social and emotional needs were to be satisfied. But, after all, we had worked so hard and come far. Only in America could such quantum leaps be taken in one generation. We had every right, or so it seemed, to expect that our children would carry us forward to new, more dazzling heights, and so we hitched our parental wagon to the filial star.

The details of this brilliant ascent were not always perfectly clear to us. When my daughter at nineteen announced that she was leaving college in order to become an actress, I didn't take to my bed.

Though in my personal dream for her, she was in Stockholm accepting the Nobel prize for biological research, or, alternately, winning the National Book Award for a brilliant first novel, I was willing to adjust my sights to an Academy Award ceremony, with my beautiful child graciously accepting her Oscar and expressing her appreciation for her mother's understanding and support. All this, of course, would be harmoniously combined—I was not sure how— with marriage and motherhood, although I could also accept her sacrifice of the career for her family. What I could not adjust to in the years after she left college was the aimlessness, the dilettantism that took her on a downward spiral from acting in minor film roles to working, in succession, as a fashion model, salesgirl, receptionist, to a long period of unemployment during which she sampled desultorily a variety of "mind expanding" experiences that included LSD, Zen, and a religious cult or two. But I did not have a "heart attack." The depression I sank into was all too real, compounded of my sense of guilt and failure. I could not understand, when I had achieved the "success" my mother had envisioned for me—that is, a decent standard of living and a university career—why it was that I could not do for my daughter what my mother, with none of my advantages, had been able to do for me. Psychologist Naomi James says: "So many young adults today lack a Self; they don't know who they are or what they want to do with their lives."

In Saul Bellow's novel *The Adventures of Augie March*, Augie says, "I touched all sides and nobody knew where I belonged. I had no good idea of that myself."

My mother knew exactly what she wanted for

me: She wanted me to be a college graduate and a wife and mother. Her methods may be open to question, but she lived to see her goals for me realized, and in her own way she helped me create my Self. I didn't have a clear and realistic set of goals for my daughter; I knew only that I wanted her to continue what began at the turn of the century in Odessa when my grandfather announced to my grandmother, "We are going to America." And when my daughter showed no interest in developing her Self through acting out my scenario, I felt she had failed me.

I could not see through the distorted view of my parental expectations that for most of us in my generation, everything had been geared to the centralized and unified mission of making a better life for us. This is what gave us the psychological space to grow in. There was never any question of competing with our parents, whose ambitions, if they had any, had been checked by the depression; compared to where they were, we had no way to go but up. But how about the generation of our children whose parents are successful achievers, suburban sophisticates who have "made it" according to the American criterion of "making it"? Is it our very "success" that has bred a generation for whom narcissism may be the only refuge from a competition they are certain they would lose and that they are not at all sure they want to win? Locked into our generational values and expectations, we measure our children by standards they can never meet. "You've let us down" is the silent reproach that speaks to them louder than words. What we often fail to see is how this wedges them into a tight spot, between the rock of our expectations and the hard place of a world of diminishing resources.

When the adult child tries to live up to the parents' standards, the emotional cost may be higher than either bargained for. A twenty-two-year-old violinist whose father is a well-known cellist described to me her ceaseless effort since she began playing the violin at the age of seven to win her father's approval. "He's such a perfectionist," she told me, "that no matter how well I played, he'd always find something wrong. One evening, when he was visiting me, a few of my string-playing friends came over and we put on an impromptu musical performance. I played a few solos—and it was all in fun and very relaxed. But I could sense my father's disapproval, especially when my friends were praising my playing. Sure enough, when my friends left my father said some disparaging things about my solos and capped it by telling me that if I listened to my adoring sycophants, I would lose my capacity for self-criticism.

"For weeks afterward, every time I thought of my father or was with him, I could feel this anger boiling up inside of me. I knew he was aware of my feelings and that he was hurting too, but we're both bullheaded and neither would make that first move.... Finally, I wrote him a letter....

" 'Why can I not have an hour or so of grace from the bog of self-criticism in which I am constantly submerged? Must I, every one of my waking moments, cast a cold, critical eye over all of my endeavors? Can I not receive praise from other up-and-coming violinists without you demeaning them and dissipating the effect of their words by calling them "adoring sycophants"? Believe me, none of

your criticism could possibly compete with my
drought-resistant reservoir of self-analysis, micro-
scopic deliberations, cell-by-cell examination, and un-
ceasing belittling assessments in the cold, white light
of that inverted shadow known as "perfection," under which both you and I are destined to live out our
lives.

" 'I have been practicing all morning. Imagining
your perfectionist eye upon me as I played two movements of the Handel, I realized that my rendition
was just this side of ghastly. So you needn't worry—
my capacity for self-critique is intact, despite my
brief moment of basking in the warmth of admiration and praise.' "

The letter was not conciliatory in tone, nor was
it intended to be, but it gave the daughter a chance
to let off steam and provided the father with an illuminating view of his rigid, uncompromising stance.
"We'll always have our problems," said the daughter
in summing up this episode, "but my letter helped us
break through to each other, and there's been a
change. My father no longer expects me to play like
Isaac Stern all the time."

The Two-Way Distortion

Parent-child expectations are not a one-way
street; they operate in both directions. Adult children
frequently express disillusionment with their parents and, as one psychologist noted, sometimes describe parents as ogres without a single redeeming
feature. A senior at Boston University spoke of his
sense of deep personal loss when he discovered, at
the age of twelve: "My father wasn't the great guy

I'd always thought he was. My two big interests at the time were nature and poetry, and I wrote my first poem about some monarch butterflies I'd been observing in the field behind our house. I took it to my English class and my teacher said she thought it was good enough to get published in the school magazine. So then I showed it to my father, and he gave me a strange look. 'Poetry,' he said. 'That's kind of a sissy thing to do.' He said, 'Maybe I haven't been spending enough time with you.' And he started taking me to prizefights, bought me a rifle and took me hunting. The first time I shot a wild duck and it landed at my feet, its neck twisted and its feathers all bloody, I ran into the woods and vomited. I was lying there crying, and my father pulled me to my feet and hit me in the face. 'I'm ashamed of you,' he said. 'From now on I expect you to act like a man.' It was a terrible crisis in my life."

In *The Managerial Woman*, a daughter recalls the moment during her adolescence when she became disillusioned with her mother. It happened when "she began to suggest that I give up my tomboy status. She said I should settle down and learn to become a young lady. . . . I looked upon myself as a person. I thought that it was unfortunate that I wasn't a boy, only because it would have made things easier for everyone. I remember blaming her for that, too."[2]

Our view of each other is distorted not only by our mutual expectations but also by our family roles as defined and sanctioned by our culture. In becoming a Mother or a Father, we are wrapped in a man-

[2]Margaret Henning and Anne Jardim, *The Managerial Woman* (New York: Pocket Books, 1978).

tle of predetermined associations, which, like a standardized garment, we are required to wear whether it suits us or not. However, any alterations must be made, not in the garment but in ourselves.

The figure of Mother has been invested with powerful mythological and symbolical qualities. She is earth and moon, fertility and fruitfulness, a repository of wisdom and solicitude, and, on the negative side, she is dark, devouring, seductive, castrating, the source of all psychic ills in her sons and daughters. How can any normal human female measure up or down to such an image? As Jung tells us, actual, living, personal mothers bear little resemblance to the image or "archetype." But the archetype has succeeded in overshadowing the living person, so that when a woman becomes a mother, whatever she was before becomes submerged in Mother with a capital "M."

Mother Images

A playful, fun-loving woman with healthy sexual appetites and a set of interests that includes politics, the stock market (she earns her living as an investment counselor), ballet, skiing, sailing, and modern art gives birth to her first child. She plans to go back to her job and continue her life as before. But something has happened to her. She has become a Mother. Biological and cultural forces are generating mysterious changes within her. If she becomes a working mother, thereby reducing the capital "M" to lower case, she is subject to frequent attacks of guilt. Her husband may offer to help out, but when it comes to the crunch, she is the one who sits by the sick child's bedside, goes to school for a conference with the child's teacher, and suffers when Kathy or Rick is not invited to the all-important birthday party, wondering whether it is because she is too busy to promote her child's social life.

Whether she goes on working or stays at home and takes up full-time motherhood—assuming she has that option—there is no time for politics, ballet, skiing, and so on. All of that will have to be put on the back burner until Kathy or Rick is weaned, or toilet trained, or old enough to go to school. And so it goes. Her friends are now mostly mothers with a child or children of the same age as hers. Their conversation centers on the endlessly absorbing details of child rearing. She enters into these conversations, trading amusing anecdotes about Kathy or Rick, trotting out her child's accomplishments, sharing concerns about feeding, toiletting, and behavior problems.

She is informed and sophisticated on the subject of Motherhood, having taken the requisite psychology and sociology classes and read all the books on the reading list. Her mother and grandmother were unaware that children had psyches and thought all a child needed was to be loved, fed, and spanked now and then, but she knows different. As a member in good standing of the secular church of Psychoanalysis, she is thoroughly familiar with the gospel according to Sigmund Freud and Melanie Klein. She has been sold on the idea that the way she treats her children will mold their behavior patterns for life. As a Role Model for her daughter, she recognizes that she must conduct herself so that the little girl will grow up to be a Whole Person—feminine but not dependent, capable of orgasmic sexual pleasure but not promiscuous. Toward this goal, she submerges herself in the growing child, producing a hybrid identity, My Daughter/Myself, from which it becomes very difficult to extract the "Myself."

As for her son, here she must walk an exceedingly fine line, guiding the boy toward an image of masculinity that combines tenderness with toughness, an aggressive drive for achievement with a sensitive appreciation of the arts. She must be loving toward him so that he will be a loving husband and father, but not *too* loving or he might develop homosexual tendencies. If she is raising her children alone, as so many women are doing today, she probably has to provide financial support, and must also find some way to compensate for the children's deprivation of a father.

Meanwhile, the children's endless demands and boundless energy drain her stamina; fatigue replaces playfulness, and sleep is what she most looks forward to in bed. When, after a particularly trying day, her husband or lover settles in bed beside her, she breathes rhythmically, imitating sleep. She is not up to a bout of lovemaking, what with having to fit in the diaphragm and the effort to act out an orgasm, in case she doesn't have one—which is more and more the way it is for her these days. Sex will simply have to be relegated to a sometime thing until the children are more self-sufficient. For the moment the Mother has edged out the Woman.

Father Images

Father, too, has his image to live up to and live with, regardless of his personal predilections. Father is a rock, a tower of strength. Whereas Mother is soft and fruitful, Father is hard and tensile. Father is the bone and muscle of the family, the breadwinner, the final court of appeal. Studies of the impact of sex roles on children conducted in the 1960s showed that children saw their mothers as love-oriented and their fathers as power-oriented, punitive, and fear-inspiring, but at the same time they thought their fathers were more competent than their mothers in dealing with the outside world.

But there is another image of Father, the mass media image, which is the extreme opposite of hard/powerful/competent. "The astounding thing in this society," says Dr. Alan Gurwitt, a psychiatrist at the Yale Child Study Center, "is that the father has come to be a subject of ridicule—there is no end to the cartoon and movie stereotypes portraying the expectant father, and fathers in general, as bumbling fools."

Father's conventional role has incorporated both of these extremes into a somewhat unlikely combination. Father has been expected to serve as the family breadwinner and, as such, to be tough, shrewd, and hard-nosed, working long hours when necessary to meet the needs of his growing family. This has kept him away from home much of the time so that he has been in effect a weekend father. Enter the bumbling fool—what else could he be seen as on the domestic front when Mother made all the important family decisions?

Father has also been expected to act as a model for Son when the boy reached manhood, as well as for Daughter's future husband. In acting out this role, Father is never to be caught in an unseemly display of emotion; tears or any show of sentiment would be considered feminine and would set a poor example of maleness. The only emotion permitted is anger. Hugging and kissing in moderation are appropriate when the children are small, but when Son and Daughter became teen-agers, displays of affection are to be kept strictly under control.

Columnist Jim Sanderson quotes from a novel by Ingrid Bengis that describes a scene in a small family restaurant in provincial Italy: "A father embraces his son, strokes his hair, kisses his mouth, holds him in his lap. A daughter scrambles up on a stool beside her father as he rings up a lunch bill on the cash register. There is a tenderness in the father's eyes that is so intimate, so natural that I gasp inwardly with pleasure, conscious that the same gestures in America would seem glaringly conspicuous." And Sanderson asks: "Why should this be so? Why does it take only a single generation for even Italian males in this country to become as stoic, as afraid of touching, as any Anglo-Saxon? Is it because of the American pioneer tradition in which men had to focus all their energies on taming a raw continent—suppressing emotional display as a sign of weakness?" And he broods over the possibility that Father may no longer know how to demonstrate affection, that the capacity to feel may have been bred out of him.

Son and Daughter Images

Son and Daughter have traditionally inspired very different sets of parental expectations. In a study of parents whose children were in their early teens during the 1960s, the parents, when talking about their sons, emphasized activity, competitiveness, and achievement. Recurring phrases were: showing ambition and backbone; having leadership qualities; being self-assured and self-sufficient. The desirable qualities for daughters were mainly in the realm of social interaction: poise, politeness, courtesy, kindness, generosity, understanding of people's problems. These middle-class parents worried if their sons did not demonstrate initiative, responsibility, assertiveness, athletic skill, emotional stability. They worried if their daughters were not attractive, charming, and popular.

Those of us whose children are now adults, some with families of their own, can surely remember how we cheered our sons on in their Little League games and pushed them hard in school, warning and threatening that if their grades weren't good enough for a "prestige college," they might as well kiss their future goodbye. And our daughters? We paid lip service to scholastic achievement. Yes, it would be fine for them to have a career, at least until they married, and if they wanted to do us proud, they would marry a man who was going places and tag along with him.

With all of this changing so rapidly, we are caught up in crosscurrents of role confusion. As the old codes of sexual behavior go into the discard, we are left with an identity vacuum that we attempt to fill with improvisations: ad hoc relationships that serve for the passing moment; therapies that promise instant mental salvation; a hedonistic preoccupation with pleasure and personal fulfillment.

In our groping efforts to make some sense out of it all, the communication circuits between us and our adult sons and daughters remain blocked. Though the images are growing blurry, we persist in looking at them as Son and Daughter, attempting to reinforce the only connection with them that we have ever known. And since we have never revealed ourselves to them as anyone other than their Parent, they continue to view us as Father and Mother, shifting archetypes that never quite come into human focus.

Phasing Out the Parent

The transition from parent to ex-parent is a developmental process that involves two stages: unlearning, or disconnecting, and relearning, or reconnecting, as we establish a new relationship with our adult children. Stage One consists of a series of self-modifying behaviors that prepare you for Stage Two.

Coming Out from Behind the Labels

What were you before you were Mother or Father? What were your interests? What did you get worked up about? How did you spend your leisure time? What did you give up "for the children" that you now wish you hadn't? One of the advantages today of being at the age when one's children are adults is that so many options are open to us, options that were not available to previous generations of people in midlife. We can now pick up where we left off in our youth, if that's what we want to do, and realize long-deferred dreams. The mature men and women who are enrolling as students at college campuses; the middle-aged career changers; the married couple in their late forties, lifetime urban dwellers, who move to the country, buy a farm, and take correspondence courses in agricultural science—these and many others like them are defying F. Scott Fitzgerald's statement, "There are no second acts in American lives." If we are willing to write our own scripts, our lives can have many acts and scene changes before curtain time.

Deritualizing Our Behavior

In emerging from parental stereotypes we have to peel away layers of arbitrary attitudes and ritualized behaviors. Parenting, like any other activity that goes on day by day over a span of years, becomes habit-forming. You develop behavior tics and reflexes, conditioned responses that control you like strings manipulated by an invisible puppeteer. Long after the reasons for the responses have vanished, the empty rituals continue. Habits, of course, can be difficult to break. But it helps if (1) you become intensely aware of the habit and its harmful effects, and (2) you make a conscious and consistent effort to change your stimulus-response behavior patterns.

Behavior to Avoid

Don't offer unsolicited advice or assistance. Assume that your adult children can solve their own problems and that if they can't, you probably can't do it for them.

Avoid any suggestion of a mother/father-knows-best stance. A posture of superior wisdom is fatal to any honest exchange of views between adults.

Don't try to manipulate the course of events in your adult children's lives. A wealthy manufacturer confessed to me that he had arranged for his daughter, upon her graduation from college, to be hired as associate editor of a magazine in which his company ran substantial advertising. He accomplished this by hinting that otherwise the advertising might be withdrawn and by surreptitiously paying her salary. "She had her heart set on that job," said the father, "and I'd always given her everything she wanted." But when the daughter found out the truth about her job, she resigned, and "from then on," her father says unhappily, "things have never been the same between us."

Resist the temptation to protect your adult children from "the slings and arrows of outrageous fortune." Once they are grown there is no way you can shield them from the hurts and pangs and disappointments of adult life. You can offer sympathy and understanding as you would to a contemporary, but that's about it. If your daughter is going through an unhappy love affair, restrain yourself from insisting that she "break it off now" when she may not be ready for that, even though you are convinced that continuing the relationship will only bring her more pain. Also, any attempt to retaliate on your adult child's behalf should be firmly suppressed. There was a memorable incident during Harry Truman's presidency, when he berated a music critic for publishing an unfavorable review of a singing performance by daughter, Margaret. It was an embarrassment for Margaret, and she would have been entirely justified in giving her father the President a severe tongue lashing.

Never, under any circumstances, make your son or daughter feel guilty for not phoning or visiting you as often as you'd like. A sense of obligation is a pathetic substitute for a genuine desire to make contact. When you have successfully reconnected, you will assume that not hearing from your children means all is well, and go about your own business. When you do hear from them, you will know they are acting out of their own volition and not because of any pressure from you.

Eliminate from your consciousness any traces of self-pity or martyrdom. "After all I've done for you—" are words that should never cross your mind or your lips. Children are usually instrumentalities of parental sacrifice—that is, the parents, in making certain "sacrifices" on behalf of the children, are seeking to fulfill themselves through the children. To construe parental self-denial as a promissory note that must be repaid on demand is like saddling someone with a debt that he or she was unaware of taking on.

Bite your tongue whenever you are tempted to make comparisons with the way it was when you were your children's age. Remove from your conversational lexicon any statement beginning with "In my day" and all such expressions as "We weren't spoiled like you—we knew what it was to do without"; "We had respect for our elders in those days"; "You used to read a book now and then—we didn't let you sit around watching TV all the time."

Unlearning the mannerisms and responses of the Parent doesn't mean that we unlearn our love for our children. What happens is that we learn to love them in a new way, not because they are ours, but because they are *they*. In reconnecting, we liberate each other from the molds that have been compressing our human selves; we are then free to come together as good friends who share a common set of memories.

4
Reconnecting: Phasing In the Friend

While our children were growing up, we did whatever we could to conceal ourselves from them. We hastily broke off conversations when they entered the room, so that they wouldn't catch us telling an off-color story or discussing the erotic passages of a best-selling book or exchanging anecdotes about our sexual experiences. We cleaned up our language and our behavior in front of the children. We tried to keep our marital discord as well as our lovemaking out of their sight and hearing.

Well, after all, we wanted their respect, admiration, and love. Could we have these if they saw us on occasion as fearful, weak, lustful, petty—in a word, human? We were afraid to risk it, secretly afraid that the Self beneath the Parent was not deserving of respect, admiration, and love. And so, while creating our children in our own image, we were also creating a false image of ourselves.

Coming Out of the Closet

The process of reconnecting begins for the parent by "coming out of the closet." It's like taking off a mask and saying, Here I am, for better or worse. You may not like everything about me, but maybe I don't like everything about you, either. And that's all right. Accepting each other for what we are doesn't mean suspending our critical judgments or abandoning our values. It simply means viewing each other compassionately, without illusions or expectations.

As you shed the label of Mother or Father, you will find that you can let down your guard and share with your adult children your beliefs, ideas, likes, dislikes, needs, wishes, anxieties, interests, attitudes. But when you do, make sure you are expressing what you really think and care about. There's no point in pandering to your children, as so many parents do, in the mistaken belief that this is the way to win their hearts and minds. Pretending that you like rock music when you detest it, or that you approve of casual sex when it offends your moral sense, or using the current jargon and four-letter words when they feel foreign to your tongue—these "put-ons" are usually transparent and rarely fool your adult children. I've heard several young adults say: "My father [or mother] is a phony. He [she] says one thing but really believes something else." And when you are caught in these inconsistencies, your adult children recognize the old manipulative tugging of the strings.

"But if we disagree with our children," parents ask, "if much of what they believe in and care about is alien to us, how can we be their friends?"

Well, why not? Do the people you consider your friends always conform to your ideas, values, and standards of behavior? I have a good friend whose political beliefs are the exact antithesis of mine. Many of our encounters are enlivened by our debates on politics; it's an ongoing dialectic that both of us thoroughly enjoy. And I notice something interesting: She is beginning to soften her views here and there with a few nuances from my side of the argument; and some of her persuasions are beginning to creep into my thinking. We are opening chinks in each other's once-solid walls of opinion—and we are not so sure anymore that, in the realm of politics, either one of us is in possession of the ultimate truth.

What we are doing, in effect, is educating each other. And we can do this, my friend and I, because of our mutual trust, respect, and enjoyment. We take as much pleasure in our differences as in our similarities. And our trust and respect are based on our longstanding honesty with each other.

The key to a solid and enduring friendship is this quality of honesty, or genuineness. Through revealing ourselves to others, we discover who we are. There is a kernel of truth in the joking question: How do I know what I think till I hear what I say? We also discover who the other person is, and to what extent we are alike and different. When we go on seeing our adult children as Son and Daughter, we are viewing them through the wrong end of the telescope, which diminishes them by the distance between where they are and where we want them to be. We don't require our friends to live out our dreams or live up to an arbitrary set of expectations. Why should we require these behaviors from our grown-up children? Seeing our sons and daughters for what they are, we see each as a separate person, familiar but, at the same time, with the capacity to surprise us.

Unmixing the Messages

The absence of genuineness is responsible for much of the dissonance in parent-child communication. In studying the mother-daughter relationship, a psychiatrist, Dr. William Pieper, maintains that mothers and daughters rarely experience a totally trusting friendship because of their inability to be completely open with each other. "The type of friendship I'm talking about," says Dr. Pieper, "is the ability of a mother and daughter to be totally available to each other. Totally trusting, caring, loving, honest, and involved." Without these qualities, which are the basic components of genuineness, the relationship is warped and neither person can be a real friend to the other.

"I was always getting mixed messages from my mother," says a thirty-five-year-old woman, who recently adopted a baby girl. "She wanted me to work hard at my studies, get good grades, be at the top of my class. But she also wanted me to be popular, to have a lot of boyfriends and invitations. She put a lot of pressure on me—but at the same time she never really talked to me. I had all these confusions and anxieties, but when I tried to discuss my feelings with her, she'd close up tight. I had to conform to her image of what *she* had wanted to be: strong, successful, sought-after. There wasn't any room in that image for feelings of doubt and insecurity. I'm hoping that I can be open and real with my daughter and accept her for what she is."

The mixed messages we send to our children usually emanate from the subbasement of our consciousness. We are simply unaware of how often we tell them one thing while acting out something entirely different. During their growing years, our children are observing and questioning the entire ethical system we represent, and are drawing their conclusions from what we do as well as what we say. A thirty-year-old woman who grew up in a replica of an English Tudor mansion in Westchester County, New York, and who describes her relationship with her parents as "distant," recalls: "My parents gave generously to the NAACP, but they treated our black cook, whom I adored, as less than human." And an artist with a studio in Manhattan's SoHo district recalls his father "making a big deal about going to Sunday school so we'd grow up to be good Christians, but he cheated his customers and was one of the most accomplished liars I've ever known."

Learning to unmix the messages is a consciousness-raising experience. It involves a high degree of self-observation and self-analysis, which, however, is very different from self-preoccupation—in fact, it is quite the opposite. To detect the gap between our words and our actions requires a certain detachment and objectivity, the ability to look at ourselves through the eyes of others. It is not an easy thing to do, to be sure, but well worth the effort; and in this we can enlist the help of our adult children by demonstrating our readiness to accept their criticism and advice.

When they were growing up, it was always *we* who advised and criticized *them*. We were the ones they looked up to—and they saw themselves reflected in our praise and criticism. But for the most part we did not encourage or take very seriously their criticism of us. As Mother or Father we enjoyed a kind of parental immunity from our children's honest opinion of us. Maybe deep down we didn't want to know what they really thought; we may have preferred to remain on the parental pedestal, even when it seemed a bit shaky at times, rather than risk being brought down to earth with a sharp jolt to our self-esteem.

There's always some risk in being open and self-revealing, and in acting upon our honest convictions. But if we go the other way and continue sending mixed messages to our adult children, we are lessening our chances of developing into the ex-parent they can count on as a friend.

What Is a Friend?

What does it mean to be a friend? What do you look for in your friends that is special to the relationship?

I put these questions to a diverse group of people, and here are some of the answers:

Fifty-five-year-old social worker, father of four grown children: "I expect my friends to be there when I need them and respect my privacy as I respect theirs."

Forty-two-year-old aerospace engineer, father of three teen-agers: "I like to be able to relax with my friends, get together after work, have a beer, talk about this and that, nothing heavy, just enjoy being together."

Twenty-one-year-old college student (male): "With my friends I want to be able to be myself. Like with a girl or your parents, you've always got to be putting on an act, you know. . . ."

Thirty-two-year-old journalist, divorced mother of a four-year-old daughter: "I once wrote these lines to a friend: 'All I can give you is the experience of myself. All you can give me is the experience of yourself.' "

Forty-eight-year-old sociology professor, mother of two grown children: "Being a friend means being able to accept the other, including the warts and pimples, to enjoy each other's small and big steps and to laugh together."

Parent and Friend: What's the Difference?

But isn't it possible, you may very well be wondering, to be a parent and a friend to your adult children at one and the same time?

Possible, but not very likely, when you consider the fundamental differences in the way we experience these two connections. To start with, the most obvious distinction: You can choose your friends but not your parents or your children, except in the case of adoption, and even there, the choice is unilateral, with the adopted children having very little to say about it.

There are other crucial differences. The parent has had a protective, nurturing relationship with the child, and therefore feels a vested interest in the child's future. Not so with the friend, who, not being responsible for the other's development, is concerned neither with the past nor the future but rather with the present state of the relationship.

Because of their emotional involvement with their children, parents take their children's problems as their own. Friends, while offering sympathy and understanding and acting as mutual helping agents, do not appropriate each other's problems.

Parents see their children as an extension of themselves. Friends accept each other for what they are.

Communication between parents and children is limited and guarded. Friends communicate freely and spontaneously, sharing thoughts, worries, enthusiasms.

How differently the two attachments manifest themselves comes through clearly when we look at how each reacts to situations like these:

Situation

Decision to leave job and attempt to find more personal satisfaction, possibly through some form of creative activity.

Parent's reaction: That's very unwise. Jobs don't grow on trees, you know. How are you going to support yourself?

Friend's reaction: I think it's a great idea, if that's what you really want to do. That job has never satisfied you. You deserve a chance to try out your talents. After all, with your background and experience, you can always get another job.

·Situation

Opportunity to work for multinational company in developing African nation.

Parent's reaction: But it's so far away! We'll never see you. I don't understand how you can even consider it.

Friend's reaction: Wow! what a challenge. And you'll be learning so much. I'll miss you—but we'll write to each other.

Situation

Thirty-eight-year-old woman, high-level corporate executive, married ten years, no children, becomes pregnant, considers abortion.

Parent's reaction: How can you do this to us? You know how much it would mean to us to have a grandchild.

Friend's reaction: Well, after all, you and Bob have never wanted the responsibility of children. As long as you're sure you won't regret it later. . . .

Situation

Couple's decision to divorce after five years of marriage.

Parent's reaction: It's no surprise to me. I told you from the beginning that he/she was spoiled, selfish, and irresponsible.

Friend's reaction: I know what you two have

been going through. I hate to see it happen, but I guess there's no other way. If there's anything I can do to help, please let me know. . . .

Taking the Risk

How do we know that the shift from parenthood to friendship, that revealing ourselves to our adult children, will be welcomed by them? What if they find it awkward and embarrassing? Supposing they'd prefer that we remain their parents instead of becoming their friends. What then?

Well, let's consider this. As adults capable of managing their own lives, your children no longer need the services that you performed for them as a parent. That role is now obsolete. You can, of course, continue clinging to an obsolete role if you choose to, but then what usually happens is that you are left at the wayside while the stream of life passes you by. If you choose to remain Father and Mother, your children will continue as Son and Daughter, and as the years go by your lives will grow farther and farther apart.

I have talked with several sophisticated professionals who cannot understand why there is this distance between them and their adult children: a woman, whose rise to personnel director of a utilities corporation is due mainly to her skill in human relations, by her own admission "simply can't get along with my son and daughter-in-law"; the dean of a liberal arts college in Minnesota, who is the adored father confessor and buddy of the eight hundred students in residence, has an awkward and cool relationship with his twenty-five-year-old son.

I heard this from a forty-five-year old power-house who heads her own public relations agency in San Francisco: "Here I am a communications expert, right? I can outtalk anyone in the business. You know what they call me in the trade? Fastest tongue in the West. So how is it, when I'm with my daughter and her husband, I can't think of anything to say? And I always come home feeling—sort of—depressed."

Before my transition to ex-parenthood, I used to have long, intimate, soul-satisfying talks with my daughter—entirely in my head. In anticipation of a visit with her, I would save up scraps of conversational material for us to share, amusing and revealing bits and pieces that would surely patch over the gaping holes of time and space that separated us. This time, I would tell myself, we will find out who we really are, how we think, how we have changed in these last years—and we'll draw together and enjoy each other as we used to. But somehow we would never have these talks. When the moment came, my courage would fail me, and I would remain within the familiar and protective shelter of Parenthood.

My mother remained a Parent to the end of her days, and our relationship after I became an adult was conducted almost entirely on the surface. Only once did I catch a glimpse of my mother's hidden self. Shortly before her death she talked about a boy she had been attracted to when she was in her teens, and how her father, a European patriarch, had discouraged the match because the boy's mother smoked cigarettes and was said to be a "loose woman," and how later, she met my father, who pursued her relentlessly until she gave in and married him, still thinking about the other boy. There was a soft brooding expression on her face as she talked about that episode in her early life; it was an expression I couldn't remember ever seeing before.

I think now that I could have breached the maternal facade and learned much that I would like to know about my mother, and that I will never know now that she is gone. But that would have meant stepping out of my role as Daughter and talking to her woman-to-woman. And that I wasn't willing to do. Over the years I had become more practiced at concealing than revealing in my relationship with my mother, and it was the path of least resistance for me to continue noncommunicating as I had been doing since my teens.

As parents of grown children, many of us can remember how the circuits of communication began closing off during our children's adolescent years when suddenly a son or daughter who was once clear and open as a summer sky turned secretive and remote. One of the fathers I interviewed said he can pinpoint the moment when this happened with his fifteen-year-old son. "It was at the tail end of the sixties. We were living in Philadelphia at the time, and my son was attending a private school in Massachusetts, not far from Boston. Sending him to that school represented a financial sacrifice for us, but we thought it was important for him, that it would give him both the freedom and the discipline he needed.

"I should tell you that my son was always a very open and outgoing boy. We had a close and affectionate relationship, and he talked freely, not only to me, but also to his mother and younger brother about his interests and experiences. When he came home for his first Christmas vacation, we realized he wasn't as enthusiastic about the school as he'd been at first, but I put it out of my mind, figuring it was just the normal ups and downs of getting accustomed to a new environment. Then one morning in March, I was in the kitchen fixing a pot of coffee when I heard a tap on the back door—and there he was, looking tired and bedraggled. I blurted out: 'What are you doing here?' and it must have sounded harsh and accusing to his ears, because that did it. He clammed up, and all we could get out of him was that he had run away from school—he'd hitchhiked to Boston and bought a plane ticket with money he'd saved—and he had no intention of going back, ever.

"Well, you can imagine how we felt. That school represented a heavy investment for us, and we thought his behavior was thoughtless and irresponsible. For the first time in our lives I played the heavy father. I argued, threatened, tossed the book at him. He took it all quietly, but he couldn't be budged. So finally I gave up and withdrew him from the school. But it was several years later—he was in college by then—before the whole story came out. There was an older boy at that school who'd been giving our son mescaline, and our boy had had a few bad trips. He'd left school because he was afraid of coming under the older fellow's influence. My reaction added to his feeling of guilt and failure—and that was what made him close up and withdraw from us."

It is often when we are caught by surprise, as this father was, that we bungle our communication with our children. A mother of grown children who is also a family counselor suggests that we try to anticipate the possible crises that might occur in our children's lives and role-play—with a spouse or friend—our reactions to these events so that we have some psychological preparation for them if and when they become a reality. We might then be better able to spare ourselves and our children the kind of trauma that brings on secrecy and withdrawal.

It doesn't, however, take a traumatic experience for children to close up and pull away from their parents during adolescence. A certain amount of withdrawal into oneself is normal and healthy during these growing years; it's part of becoming a separate person with one's own private thoughts and feelings. But when the practice of parent/child secrecy and concealment persists into the adult years, it can bring on mistrust and estrangement, and the longer it continues, the more difficult it is to break the pattern. At some point the parent must take the risk and shift to another level of communication—the level of friendship.

A woman I know, a divorced mother of three who is the advertising director of a large department store, told me how she made the leap over the communication gap between herself and her eighteen-year-old daughter. But the story starts two years earlier when the daughter was sixteen and the mother discovered how little she knew about the person she felt closest to in all the world:

"I remember how shocked I was when I found out that my daughter had been sexually active since she was fourteen. I'd had her boyfriend over to the house many times. They studied together and I thought it was all very sweet—and here she was, putting on this innocent act for two years and I never suspected. What was happening here was—my daughter is very religious . . . I come from a religious background, I don't make a big deal about it, but my daughter has absorbed my religious values, and she was afraid that if she told me, I would be deeply hurt. There are some children," the mother added, "who hold back out of fear of retaliation. Mine"— and there was a note of pride in her voice—"have kept things from me out of regard."

She paused, reflecting, and went on. "I *was* deeply hurt, and I didn't know how to handle it. Even though I understood her reasons, it upset me to think that she would exclude me from such an important experience in her life. I felt I couldn't trust her. You know, it never occurred to me at the time that I'd never told her much about *my* personal life. Anyway, a little coolness developed between us. I didn't know how to reach her, and she didn't seem to be trying to reach me. And then one day she had just graduated from high school and it was summer vacation and we were in the car on the way to Stratford in Connecticut to attend a performance at the Shakespeare Theatre there. It was a long drive from where we lived in New York, and I remember thinking that this was the first time in years that we'd had hours together just by ourselves—and we began talking and something happened. There was a lot of sharing and closeness, and she started crying, and she said she'd been carrying something in her heart for two years that she wanted to tell me—she'd had an abortion when she was sixteen. It was just about the time I'd found out that she was sexually active. She wanted to tell me then, but she couldn't bring herself to it, she felt she'd hurt me enough. . . .

"Well, there I was driving the car, and she was crying and feeling guilty and miserable—and I decided to take a big risk. I told her I'd had an abortion, too, a couple of years after my divorce. And yes, I'd suffered terrible guilt over it, especially since our religion regarded what I'd done as a mortal sin. And I said I thought what she'd done had taken a lot of courage, going through that experience alone.... It felt as though we were having our first mature conversation, two women sharing something important.

"I had this need to tell her because, otherwise, I was afraid she might feel later on that she'd been put at a disadvantage. You know how it is, how you can spill your guts and afterward feel simply terrible and wish you'd kept your mouth shut. I wanted to equalize things between us, I wanted to change our relationship. And I think that was the turning point for us, because since then there's been a lot of sharing between us. I think she knew that what I'd told her meant a great deal to me; I wasn't just tossing her something in return for what she'd given me. It was our mutual vulnerability that made us see each other in a new way.

"What's been happening is that now I can allow myself to worry out loud, whether it's about my job or the relationship I'm having with a man—and she gives me advice. She shares her point of view with me, and I listen to her—and it's been like adding a whole new dimension to my life. I am constantly amazed at her, at her insights, her sensitivity to people. And it's given her a lot of strength and confidence, that I not only listen to her—I act on her advice."

This may be the critical test of ex-parenthood—being ready not only to listen to our adult children, but to act on their advice when it makes sense for us to do so. It may seem difficult at first to accept advice from those to whom we have always been guide and counselor. But as Margaret Mead has shown, we have been steadily moving from what she calls a "postfigurative" culture, in which children learn primarily from adults, to a "prefigurative" culture, in which adults learn also from the children.[1] The era through which we are living and the future we are facing cannot be mapped by our past experience. Whereas, in fundamental respects, our world may have resembled that of our parents and grandparents, the world of our children and their children will in no way resemble ours. The children we have reared may be the guides who are best equipped to steer us toward the unknown future.

---

[1]Margaret Mead, *Culture and Commitment: A Study of the Generation Gap* (New York: Natural History Press/Doubleday & Co., Inc., 1970).

PART II

A Difference in Values

The fateful act of living in and with one's generation
completes the drama of human existence . . .
　　　　　　　　—Martin Heidegger, *Time and Being*

5
The Great Divide

There has probably never been a time when raising children has been entirely free of conflict and confusion. But the parents whose children were growing up during the period from the fifties to the seventies experienced a series of psychological shocks and disruptions unlike anything that had ever happened before between older and younger generations. In previous eras intergenerational differences took place within recognized boundaries. The son of the town's wealthiest man might marry the daughter of a poor laborer—a scenario familiar in fact and fiction—but both subscribed to the same social code. Once the girl learned to dress and speak "properly," she could be absorbed into middle- or even upper middle-class life and would soon be indistinguishable from her more privileged kinfolk. In his play *Pygmalion,* George Bernard Shaw showed how, in a society far more class-conscious than ours, a Cockney flower

85

girl could, by aping upper-class speech and learning a few social graces, pass herself off as a duchess.

The gaps that existed between my mother and me were, in retrospect, not the great yawning chasms they seemed at the time. I could not adopt her religious orthodoxy, which seemed to me not so much religion in any spiritual sense as a mindless adherence to ritual. I rejected her bigotry, her narrow morality, her unswerving allegiance to the principle "My family, right or wrong."

But somewhere underneath these deviations from her belief system was a solid underpinning of values that we shared. I shared her respect for education and the life of the mind; her view of sex as providing the greatest satisfaction within marriage and the family; her personal priorities, which placed the welfare of the children before parental pleasure or fulfillment; her conviction that there is a cosmic force to which we are ultimately accountable—for her it was God, for me a divine mystery.

A New Subculture

But between my generation of parents and our children, there were few, if any, common values to bridge the cavernous gaps that opened up between us somewhere during the early to midnineteen sixties. The causes and manifestations of the momentous social upheaval at that time have been and will continue to be debated for many years to come. The list includes: the Beatles, Vietnam, the rebellion against all forms of authority, the civil rights movement, television, movies, the musical *Hair*, the decline of literacy, Timothy Leary, Lenny Bruce, permissiveness, the rising divorce rate, the erosion of the family, working mothers, the New Left, women's liberation, the drug culture, motorcycles, the assassination of President Kennedy, James Dean, Jesus cults, Oriental mysticism—and on and on.

Whatever the historians finally settle on, those of us whose children were reaching puberty then remember vividly what it felt like. It was as though our world had suddenly been turned upside down, and we knew somehow it would never be the same again. Says Bill Loud, the father of the brood whose domestic trials were documented in the TV series *An American Family*: "From five to fifteen the kids were a delight. From fifteen to nineteen it was absolute hell. During the Santa Barbara antiwar riots I started feeling the world was going absolutely crazy."

We are beginning to understand what happened even if we are not sure exactly why. A new subculture emerged that Kenneth Keniston has defined as "youth"; this new stage of life follows adolescence and precedes the assumption of adult responsibilities.[1] Somewhere along the way adolescence merges into "youth," and, as we've seen, is prolonged far into the time that used to be considered the period of adulthood.

The development of this new youth culture, with its distinctive language, dress, religion, politics, and

[1]Historian G. Stanley Hall first used the word "adolescence" to refer to a new stage of life that emerged at the turn of the century; it represented the period after childhood, but before the taking on of adult responsibilities, and was applied to those children who did not go directly into the labor force but continued on into high school.

morality ripped to shreds the connecting tissue between parents and children. There were no longer
recognizable boundaries to contain the rebellion of
the younger generation against their parents. It was
more than a rebellion; it was a wholesale reordering
and restructuring of the way we and generations before us had lived. As parents of this generation of
"youth," we were unprepared to cope with the radi-
cal revision of our world; and none of what we had
tried to pass on to our children seemed to have any
"relevance," to use one of the buzzwords of the time.

Old and New Values

We discard our history so rapidly that the sixties
are beginning to seem like a quaint era in the far-
away past. Some of the "new values" that appeared
so revolutionary at the time have been absorbed into
the mainstream. We can get a clearer picture of this
phenomenon by placing the two sets of values side
by side:

Traditional Values (presixties)	*New Values (postsixties)*
Emphasis on money and status.	Emphasis on self-knowledge and self-fulfillment.
Adherence to Protestant ethic—hard work, deferred gratification.	Rejection of Protestant ethic—pursuit of pleasure—instant gratification.
Conformity to an accepted social code. Concern for family, job, society.	Nonconformist. Flexible. Primary concern with the self.

Clearly defined sex roles.	Blurring of sex roles.
Discipline in children's upbringing.	Permissiveness in child raising.
Importance of personal merit.	Importance of personality.
Strict code of sexual behavior.	Casual attitude toward sex.
Oriented toward goals. Upwardly mobile.	Aimless, drifting, "going with the flow."
Respect for heritage, tradition.	Focus on the present, readiness to experiment.
Intolerance of deviations from established norms.	Acceptance of deviant behavior. Rapidly changing norms.

Between these two sets of values is an invisible boundary line marking the Great Divide, which is actually a split in our consciousness. Our normal consciousness, says Robert E. Ornstein in *The Psychology of Consciousness,* "is our whole world," and we can consider it successful "to the extent that it enables us to survive." But we make the mistake, Ornstein adds, of believing that our personal consciousness *is* the world and that it perfectly represents reality. He illustrates this with a story of the father who says to his double-seeing son, "Son, you see two instead of one." The son replies, "How can that be? If I were, there would seem to be four moons up there in place of two."

We and our adult children have been living on either side of the Divide, experiencing separate realities that have been forged in the crucibles of our very different life experiences. Our side of the boundary line represents the consciousness of those who grew up in a preaffluent era, a world in which, as John Kenneth Galbraith reminds us, "poverty was the all-pervasive fact" for the majority of people. On the other side are those whose consciousness was shaped by the postwar affluence that made the American Dream come true for a substantial percentage of Americans. A yeasty economy, the growth of homeownership through the GI bill and other forms of federal aid, a sound currency, an expanding middle class, a faith in America's power and prestige—these were the building blocks of the value structure that dominated the consciousness of the seventies. If the economic struggle was no longer a fact of life, it was no longer necessary to adhere to values of self-discipline and self-denial. What was the point of putting off for tomorrow what should be enjoyed today when tomorrow would be taken care of by pension plans, government largesse, and the promise of an ever-expanding future?

I heard a twenty-six-year-old woman describe what she identified as the critical difference between her generation and that of her parents as follows: "My friends and I take things and people as they come; we don't make judgments according to some abstract standard of right and wrong. Our parents are so moralistic—they're always worrying about the future; they worry about what will happen to us if we're not married or earning a certain income by a certain age. We're living for now, we're not interested in the past or the future. We don't make grandiose plans, we're satisfied with small goals. . . ."

Merging Realities

Although the Great Divide is mainly a youth-maturity split, there has been a mixing and merging of values that crosses generational lines. The fact is that in a complex and dynamic society like ours, boundaries are rarely firm and fixed. As Robert Jay Lifton sees it, the boundaries within which orderly change could take place are vanishing and are being replaced by "new, fluid, threatening, liberating, confusing, revitalizing, personal boundaries."[2] The unexpected twists and turns of the values we live by have produced paradoxes and reversals in parent-child relationships.

Here are two families that represent, respectively, the traditional and the new values. Fred and Betty Birdwell grew up on neighboring family farms in Iowa. They were childhood friends and both were determined to escape from the struggle and drudgery of farm life. Over the objections of his family, Fred left for Chicago the day after his high school graduation and worked his way through the university, majoring in economics. When he graduated, he was hired as a management trainee by a company manufacturing business machines. By this time he and Betty were married and had begun the vertical ascent through the corporate hierarchy that took them, during the child-rearing years, from Chicago to New York to Dallas to Detroit, back to Chicago, and finally to Los Angeles, where Fred, as vice-president in charge of marketing, has achieved sufficient up-

[2]Robert Jay Lifton, *Boundaries: Psychological Man in Revolution* (New York: Vintage Books, 1969).

wardness to be granted an indefinite reprieve from mobility.

Not for a moment during their upward climb have they swerved from their fidelity to the values of hard work, thrift, reward for merit, and a traditional family life. Betty enjoyed being a full-time wife and mother and never gave a thought to a career. How could she have, in any case, with all that moving around? Besides, Fred was doing well enough financially; there was no need for her to earn money. And what job could be more important and more satisfying than raising children?

Betty threw herself into the job with energy and enthusiasm. She coped cheerfully with the task of establishing a home in a new location every three or four years, maintained a pleasant and orderly home atmosphere in neighborhoods with good schools, served nutritionally balanced meals, chauffeured the children to Little League and music lessons and dentists and pediatricians, and saw to it that there were good books at home and that table manners were strictly observed at mealtime.

They have been married now for twenty-four years, and if you were to catch a glimpse of them on a typical Sunday afternoon in the brick-tile-redwood backyard of their Spanish-style house overlooking the Pacific, with Betty turning the shish kebabs on the barbecue and Fred sprawled beside the pool in a welter of Sunday papers, you would say: Ah yes, there they are, inheritors of the American Dream. And so they are. Except that the dream hasn't turned out exactly as they'd expected. Their twenty-two-year-old son, Larry, when last heard from, was on his way to Venezuela as a member of a religious cult. Their twenty-year-old daughter, Jenny, had an abortion when she was seventeen, dropped out of college, and is now living with a rock musician in San Francisco.

Fred and Betty don't talk about their children very much. They make a show of shrugging the situation off. "That's how kids are nowadays." But if you prod them, they'll reveal something of how hurt they are, how incomprehensible it is to them that their adored and once adoring children turned out this way. "Not only did we give them everything," they'll tell you, "but we tried our best to keep up with their ideas. We even smoked pot with them a couple of times, though it went against our grain."

Family number two presents a milieu very different from the Birdwells'. Mark and Stella Harris are free-lance journalists who met when they were teamed up by a national magazine to do a series on communes. They describe themselves as "early beatnik," have always scorned the accumulation of possessions, decried the materialism of the society around them, and in their personal as well as professional lives have become identified with an anti-Establishment stance and a search for "alternatives."

They live in a rented mobile home in northern California and talk about giving up free-lancing and starting a weekly newspaper. They realize it's a risk, even more so than free-lance writing, in which they have established reputations. But after all, their only child, twenty-five-year-old Peter, is on his own now and doing very well. They suppose they should be pleased about him, but in fact they are—well, chagrined. Like the Birdwells, they don't understand how their child could have turned out the way he did. "I mean, there he is," Stella says wonderingly, "married ... owns his own house ... and they have a mi-

crowave oven and a color TV, all the things Mark
and I never gave a damn about. And"—as if this
were the final indignity—"he belongs to the chamber
of commerce and votes Republican!"

Adopting the New Values

In their commitment to the traditional values of
their rural Iowa upbringing, the Birdwells belong to
a rapidly diminishing American sector. According to
a nationwide survey, by 1977 more than 80 percent of
Americans, in adjusting to the realities of a changing
world, had accepted the new values or some hybrid
form of the old and the new. Along with our adult
children we began seeking self-fulfillment through
creativity and sports. We subscribed to the notion
that everyone has a "creative potential," whether it
is expressed through macramé, gourmet cooking, or
tennis. We believed, as does psychologist Abraham
Maslow, that in "the hierarchy of needs," once the
"lower" needs—physical survival and security—
have been met, the tendency is to move on to the upper levels, culminating in "self actualization." We
did what we could to help our children actualize
themselves so that they would develop into discrim-
inating consumers of the amenities that we believed
our world would continue to provide in ever-increasing abundance.

Somehow we overlooked the fact that self-fulfillment is an even more elusive goal than money and
status; we didn't consider the essential contradiction
between the pursuit of creativity, which requires
self-discipline and dedication, and the desire for instant gratification. And our view of the future did

not include a decline in American prestige and power, and a world of shortages, shrinking resources, and runaway inflation.

We congratulated ourselves in the seventies on the narrowing of those cavernous generational gaps that had opened during the sixties. After all, we in midlife were also seeking self-fulfillment and exploring our creative potential. And weren't we and the young now jogging together, wearing similar clothes and hair styles, going to the same movies, eating the same organic foods from the health stores, taking the same yoga classes, agreeing on the need to protect the environment, and so on? In sharing so many interests and activities with the young, we felt we were at the same time extending our own youth.

And so we leaped over what was left of the generation gap, landing on the other side in our tight-fitting Levis, our hair flowing in the wind, our vocabulary liberally sprinkled with "wows" and "farouts," or whatever the youth jargon happened to be at the moment. Some of us discovered that our twenty-five- or thirty-year-old marriages were stifling our creative potential, and we traded them in for swinging and group sex and encounter sessions. There were those who switched careers along with mates and gave up carpeted offices in executive suites to grow organic vegetables or fashion ceramic pots. It was a heady experience, and with our children grown and gone or nearly grown and soon to go, what an exhilarating way to fill an empty nest! We were either pushed into instant ex-parenthood or we raced toward it eagerly, impatient to savor the joys of our new freedom.

In our rush to adopt the new values, we relinquished whatever shreds of authority we may have been clinging to in our relationship with our adult children. By imitating their behavior we put our stamp of approval on it. It was a sometimes desperate attempt to reconnect quickly without going through the gradual process of growth that is involved in disconnecting and reconnecting.

As a result, profound generational differences persist. We are learning that changing our values is not as simple as changing our clothes or hair style. Those of us whose formative years took place in an earlier preaffluent era have retained in our consciousness stubborn residues of the old values, of adherence to an ethical system drawn from the Judeo-Christian tradition, together with a set of principles loosely lumped together as "Americanism." Formerly, when change occurred more slowly, it was possible for older generations to adapt to the changing consciousness of the time, and to accept the fundamental differences in thought and behavior that this brought about.

But with today's high-speed rate of change, the adaptations must be made more quickly than most of us can manage. Changing one's entire view of the world takes time and for many of us is simply impossible within our lifetime. And so, while we may be able to accept living together without marriage, we are dismayed when our daughter prefers a woman as her lover rather than a man. We may be able to share a joint with our children, but we are horrified when they go on to cocaine or PCP. And while we may not object when our adult child converts from the religious faith into which we were born to another established religion, we are shocked and bewildered when that child joins a religious cult.

We are beginning to realize that the dislocations and disorientations of our time are part of the price that we are paying for the new values. The price that is being exacted is perhaps most evident in two areas of acute concern to parents of adult children—religious cults and the use of drugs. Here, where the transition from parent to ex-parent meets what may be its severest test, the old and new values diverge, and the generations stare at each other uncomprehendingly across the Great Divide.

That New-Time Religion

In the value system of many middle-aged, middle-class Americans, religion occupies a somewhat ambiguous position. On the one hand our secular and scientific society, by encouraging skepticism, erodes the faith on which traditional beliefs and practices are based. On the other hand a materialistic society produces a sense of spiritual emptiness and meaninglessness, a need for a kind of experience that transcends the dailiness of getting and spending.

Many of us who broke away from our parents' orthodoxies have resolved this ambiguity by treating religion as a comfortable, quasi-social aspect of our lives. We have been less interested in a strict chapter-and-verse interpretation of doctrine than in the broad ethical and cultural features of our religious associations. If we sent our children to Sunday school, it was because of some vague notion that it would be good for them, like taking spiritual vitamins, to know something about the Bible and their religious heritage. We looked upon religion for our children as a wholesome all-American activity that, we hoped, would help to inculcate sound principles of living, somewhat like Little League or the Girl Scouts.

From this perspective we were totally unprepared to deal with a child who took religion seriously. One of the women I interviewed, who comes from an assimilated Jewish background, told me how distraught she was when her daughter married a Hasidic rabbi. "It seems so alien to me," she said, "so medieval. When I think of my daughter wearing a wig and taking ritual baths—I just can't relate to it. In our family we don't associate Jewishness with those strict, orthodox rituals." And she admitted she would have felt more comfortable if her daughter's husband were from another religion, as long as he wasn't really "religious."

As progressive-minded, educated parents, we were certainly not prepared for the religious cults that emerged during the past decade at a time when our children were in that interim stage of prolonged adolescence or "youth," the period of greatest susceptibility to cultism. My daughter's flirtation with the cults was brief and fleeting, for which I have been deeply grateful. But there are parents who have watched helplessly as their children "disappeared" in the wake of strange and sinister Pied Pipers. It took the tragedy of Jonestown to impress upon a horrified public the full and dangerous dimension of religious cults.

The term "cult" has been given various interpretations. The most commonly accepted view of a religious cult is that it is composed of a group of people, mostly young, who are involved in intense relationships as followers of a powerful leader who embodies a set of formal doctrines. The cults that have attracted the largest number of followers in recent years are the Children of God, the Unification Church of the Reverend Sun Myung Moon, the Krishna Consciousness movement, the Divine Light Mission, and the Church of Scientology. An important distinction between groups like these and the established churches is that cult members are recruited, often through coercion, whereas one is either born into an established religion or goes through a voluntary process of conversion in order to join it.

Profile of a Cultist

The majority of those who join cults are between eighteen and twenty-two years of age at the time of their first exposure. For many of these young people, joining a cult coincided with a period of depression and confusion, when they were suffering from a pervasive sense of life's meaninglessness, and the cults seemed to offer firm answers and a structured life.

Psychologists and psychiatric social workers identify what they refer to as a "cult indoctrination syndrome" by the following:

- Sudden, drastic alteration of the individual's value hierarchy, including abandonment of previous academic and career goals. The changes are sudden and drastic rather than the gradual ones that result from education or the maturing process.

- Reduction of learning ability and mental flexibility. The individual answers questions mechanically, substituting stereotyped cult responses for his or her own.

- A narrowing and blunting of the emotions. Feelings of affection are repressed. The individual appears emotionally flat and lifeless.

- Regression of behavior to childlike levels. The individual becomes dependent on the cult leaders and expects them to make all decisions for him or her.

- Physical changes, including weight loss and deterioration in physical appearance and expression.

- Possible pathological symptoms, including dissociation, delusional thinking and various other types of thought disorder.

The Parent-Child Schism

There is no shortage of theories to account for the emergence and growth of the cults during the past decade. Meyer Lightman, director of a cult clinic in Los Angeles that he established to assist parents of cultists, points out that the type of religious extremism represented by cults is not new, that it has occurred throughout history, particularly at times of rapid change and upheaval. The decline of magic and myth in children's lives is suggested as a causal factor by Christopher Lasch: "Formerly religion, myth and fairytale retained enough childlike elements to offer a convincing view of the world to a child. Science cannot take their place. Hence the widespread regression among young people to magical thinking of the most primitive kind; the fascination with witchcraft and the occult, the belief in extrasensory perception, the proliferation of primitive Christian cults."[3] The decline of the family and of the strong father (most cult leaders present themselves as father figures) are also offered as explanations.

But theories and explanations, however reasonable and convincing, are of little help to parents whose grown children have become members of a cult. "Unless it happens to you, you can't possibly imagine the anguish of losing a son or a daughter to one of the extremist cults" is the way a parent, who is a New Jersey physician, expressed it.

Features of the cults that are particularly nightmarish for parents are the brainwashing and mind control; severing of ties with family and friends and complete isolation from the outside world; relinquishing of all possessions; rejection of all previous values, beliefs, and goals in favor of the doctrines and priorities of the cult; assumption of a new identity, which often includes a new name; total submission of one's personal will to the leader and unquestioning obedience to the leader's orders. The result is often a schism between parent and child that becomes so deep that, as Lightman says, "The child looks at the family as evil or alien, and the family, seeing the child's behavior as freakish, feels guilty and desperate."

[3]Christopher Lasch, *The Culture of Narcissism* (New York: Warner Books, 1979).

How Could This Happen to Us?

To most Americans who are parents of grown children the cults represent something so alien and bizarre, so utterly incomprehensible that it is as if their children had suddenly sprouted horns and begun speaking in tongues. "How could an intelligent boy like my son," a cult member's father demanded, "a boy who has had a good education and a good home life—how could he fall for that sanctimonious garbage? It's such an obvious con game—oh very smooth, very slick, I grant you, but still.... That leader, who claims to have a direct pipeline to God, he's made himself a fortune and he's convinced the kids that their parents are in league with Satan."

"My daughter has had a religious upbringing," says the mother of a Moonie. "I don't understand how all those years of absorbing the values of our religion can be wiped out in a few weeks by this cult."

Why does it happen? Could it be that, so busy were we pursuing "the good life," providing our children with balanced meals and vitamin supplements, with good schools and team sports, with ballet and music lessons, orthodontia, and psychological counseling, with sports cars and surfing equipment, that we were somehow unable to help them in their quest for purpose and meaning? Nor did they receive much assistance from the world around them. A society that places its faith in a steady race for an ever-better standard of living, in the uplifting effects of consumer goods, is unlikely to provide its young, especially those who have not experienced deprivation, with an ideal that they can consider worth living for. In addition, the failure to develop a secure identity and the postponement of adult responsibilities have placed the young in a state of limbo, in which they have been prime prospects for the new messiahs holding forth seductive visions of selfless commitment and sacrifice for a "higher cause."

What Can Be Done?

The cult's insistence on its immunity to the usual legal controls on the basis of its "religious" status has increased the sense of helplessness that parents feel as they attempt to cope with what they see as a serious threat to their children's lives. A mother whose minor-age daughter was recruited by a cult speaks of her anger: "To think that a part of our society can live this way and actually force themselves upon others, particularly a child of fourteen, use her sexually, and continually feed her all these drugs, and that as parents you're not able to do anything about it, really." Said another parent of a cultist: "On top of everything else you're made to feel that your failure as a parent is what's responsible for driving your child into the cult."

Putting parents on the defensive by linking the child's participation in a cult to parent-child problems further weakens the parental position. While it is true that personal and family problems are often a factor in attracting the young to the cults, a sense of guilt can make parents feel impotent in the face of their anxiety about their child's welfare. Whatever the problems, they are more likely to be aggravated than resolved by cult membership.

The cult clinic established in Los Angeles by Meyer Lightman is, according to its director, attempting to help parents gain a perspective on the

situation. Parents who come to the clinic are usually
those whose children have joined a cult very recently. Lightman describes these parents as frightened
and confused. In meeting and talking with other parents who are going through the same experience,
they come to understand that what has happened is
not something unique to them, and some of the guilt
and anxiety is alleviated. As they emerge from their
emotional turmoil, they can begin to think about positive ways to deal with the problem.

These ways might include deprogramming or
such legal remedies as a tort action on the child's behalf for damages sustained while in the cult; a criminal action against the cult leaders, charging them
with unlawful imprisonment; conservatorship, available in California and several other states, enabling
parents to seek a court order for the removal of a
child over the age of eighteen.

Counselors who have had experience in this area
recommend that parents make every effort to stay in
communication with their children while the children
are in the cult, and avoid the parental tendency to
adopt an accusatory or guilt-inducing tone. Above
all, never give up on a child; there is always the
chance that one day the child will leave the cult, and
when that happens, he or she should know that the
parents are there, available and ready to help in
whatever way they can. At this time both parents
and children may need psychological counseling. The
situation is fraught with anxieties and emotional tensions lying just below the surface, threatening to
erupt at any moment, and these may be more than
either parent or child is able to handle alone. For this
reason it is usually advisable for ex-cultists to under-

go a "cooling off" period before resuming their former activities.

A former cult member who succeeded in picking up her life where she had left it off, reentering the university as a graduate student, wrote to her mother that the hardest part of it all was giving up her big dream of dedicating herself to a cause. Her mother's reply, of which an excerpt follows, seems to me to combine understanding, sympathy, and support in exactly the right proportions.

"Maybe your problem is having just one big dream. Try giving yourself to a whole bunch of little human-size dreams that have a chance of coming true. Dream that you are reading to a very old lady in a nursing home, and suddenly the cracked lips part in a smile and you catch a glimpse of a shy young girl peering out from behind the cataracts and the wrinkles. Or dream that you have been campaigning to save a piece of woodland, and one day when you are walking in the woods, a golden-brown goshawk swoops down, lands on your arm, cocks his head, and winks at you. Or dream of the set of Beethoven records I am sending you and of the many euphoric moments you and old Ludwig will be having together.... These are the dreams that can make our days full and happy and more than compensate for the loss of that Big Dream that is almost certain to collapse one day, leaving behind only the bitter taste of disillusion."

Preventive Measures

Since the young are often lured into the cults by their need for a cause to identify with or a group to belong to, parents may have to give this need a higher priority during their children's growing years. There are any number of community activities in which children can become involved and through which they can develop a sense of social commitment. Parents may have to make an effort to reverse the preoccupation with the self that grew to outsize proportions during the seventies—coinciding, not so coincidentally, with the growth of the cults.

Also, just as we warn children against such physical dangers as speeding on freeways or hitch-hiking, we may have to alert them to the mental dangers inherent in the ideologies of the cults. In the process of becoming ex-parents, we can share our views on these issues with our children, emphasizing the need to examine ideas carefully and critically so that they will be better able to evaluate intelligently the doctrines of any one group and reject those that appear to be spurious.

Turning On and Off

When you think about it coolly and realistically, it isn't, after all, so mind-boggling that the use of drugs has become widespread in a generation shaped by the new consciousness. Shifting moral standards, a disregard for past or future, a preoccupation with the self, the demand for instant gratification—put these things all together and you have a person who will try any experience offering a "quick fix" and a new sensation. Add to this mix an environment in which business and social activities float on a sea of alcohol, and in which there is a constant flow of messages from the media offering fast, fast relief for all sorts of disorders and discomforts by simply taking this pill or that potion, and there it is—an ideal climate for the development of a drug culture, especially among the impressionable young.

But of course the problem is much more complicated than that. As with the problem of cults, there is a good-sized inventory of psychological and sociological explanations for drug abuse by young adults: alienation; personal and family problems; pressures to compete at school or on the job; lack of purpose and a feeling of meaninglessness; the desire to escape from the difficulties and letdowns of everyday reality.... The list has by now become overly familiar, and could just as well be applied to cult membership. Other parallels between cult membership and drug abuse are the aftereffects, which include a sense of emptiness and withdrawal from normal activities and relationships; regressive behavior; physical and mental deterioration; loss of will and vulnerability to control by others.

The use of drugs by both young and old is also partly attributable to a new kind of conformity. In choosing your poison, you align yourself with this or that group, characterized by age, tastes, and social preferences. In the sixties drug taking represented a statement of protest by the rebellious young against the Establishment. Today, though narcissism has replaced social protest and marijuana has replaced the dry martini among a growing number of the middle-aged, smoking pot is still an identifying mark of the young hipster, and peer pressure continues to do its part as an ally of the pushers.

I have talked with parents whose teen-age and adult children smoke pot regularly, and most of them feel the same sort of helplessness as the parents of cultists feel. "There's nothing I can do," said a mother of five, whose ages range from sixteen to twenty-four. "If I don't let them smoke it in the house, they'll turn on at their friends' houses or out in the street. It's really out of my control. I just hope they won't get busted and that it won't harm them too much physically. As long as they don't get involved with the heavy stuff, I'm not going to worry about it."

Getting involved with the heavy stuff is the specter that haunts today's parents of adult or near-adult children. That their fears are well founded is borne out by a National Institute on Drug Abuse survey which shows that in 1979, 68 percent of young adults had tried marijuana and a third had experimented with harder drugs. By comparison, in 1962 only 4 percent of Americans aged eighteen to twenty-five had smoked marijuana and only 3 percent had tried cocaine, heroin, or hallucinogens. The ready availability of drugs, despite all the laws, gives parents a feeling of defenselessness against a growing and terrifying threat. When pushers operate freely in high school corridors and on college campuses, how much weight, we wonder, can our pleas and arguments carry?

Why Did It Happen?

The big shocker for so many parents whose children joined the spaced-out age has been the discovery that it could happen to "people like us." We have been shaken out of the comfortable routine of our lives and forced into a reassessment of much that we have lived by and held valuable. And we have been asking questions, especially the classic question for parents of our generation: Why—when we've done everything we were supposed to and followed all the rules—why did this happen?

There are more questions than answers in this worrisome business of drug usage by the young, and results of research in the medical, psychological, and sociological areas are far from definitive. It is not even entirely clear how much the parent-child relationship enters into the picture. Are intergenerational conflicts a causal factor? How about genetics? Does the DNA code explain why some are drawn to drugs and others are not? The available evidence is inconclusive, though it's clear that parents can play a role in helping a child overcome drug addiction.

In my search for clues to help me cope with some of my own confusions, I came across two families whose experiences should strike responsive chords among parents whose grown children have been or are presently in the grip of a drug problem. One family—I'll call them Emily and Bob Coleman— live in a comfortable middle-class home in a small midwestern town and are the parents of six children. The other family are the Hamiltons, better known as film and television star Carol Burnett and her husband, Joe. They live in a Beverly Hills mansion and are the parents of eleven children, eight of them from Joe Hamilton's previous marriage.

These are their stories:

The Coleman Story

It all began, the Colemans believe, when their oldest child, twenty-one-year-old Dan, was a senior at college. As his parents describe him, he was intense and ambitious and had his sights set on law school. The Colemans were proud of their son and made no secret of the fact that they expected him to go far, as a lawyer and eventually further. This was Bob's fond hope: "I saw him going into politics and—who knows—maybe one day running for Congress or something like that. It's something I always wanted to do but I never had the opportunity."

During his visits home Dan spent most of his time in his room with his door closed, studying, preparing for the LSAT's, the law-school entrance exams. One time, when his mother was cleaning his room, she noticed a bottle of pills on his desk. "Vitamins," Dan replied when she asked him what they were. "Later we found out they were amphetamines," she said. "He was taking speed to bring up his energy level, and he was also taking tranquilizers to control the anxiety attacks he was having about getting into law school.

"About this time his personality began changing. He became moody and withdrawn. He'd always been serious and introspective, but this was different. We talked about it, Bob and I, but decided it was nothing to worry about. We wrote it off as a passing phase. When you have six children from the early teens to the twenties, you don't have time to worry about the changing moods of any one of them."

Looking back, Emily and Bob remember several times when Dan tried to talk about something that seemed to be troubling him. "But the way it came out, it was confusing; we couldn't make sense out of it. We thought one time he was saying he didn't think he wanted to go to law school—after graduation he wanted to take a year off and just 'bum around.' I've never seen Bob so furious. He was practically yelling at the top of his lungs about 'irresponsibility' and 'letting us all down.' Dan looked sick and I was in tears. What we didn't realize was that by this time our son was hooked. Drugs were a way of life for him, and he was pushing the stuff to get the money for what he needed.

"Of course, he failed the law-school entrance exams and after that he dropped out of our lives. We lost track of him, didn't know where he was, whether he was dead or alive. Bob said he didn't care, but I didn't believe him. You never stop caring. I think now if we had stayed in touch with Dan during that difficult senior year, maybe things would have been different. He was going through all sorts of painful experiences—the relentless competition at college and his first serious love affair with a girl who rejected him—but we weren't tuned in to any of that. We weren't hearing anything we didn't want to hear."

Dan suddenly reappeared in the Coleman's lives when they were notified that he'd been arrested on a drug charge. "The ultimate horror," Emily says. "Our brilliant, sensitive son—in jail! But today—can you believe it?—we're grateful for that. . . . It's what saved him."

Today, Dan is drug-free, works for a publishing company, and lives with a girl he thinks he might marry one day. What brought about this miracle? The Colemans attribute it partly to the one-year sentence in a correction camp: "The forced confinement was a shock treatment for all of us." But a good share of the credit must go to their determined effort to move beyond their parental aspirations and disappointment to an appreciation of their son for what he is rather than what they wanted him to be.

During his recovery, they completed the shift from parent to ex-parent: "And there we were, having real conversations for the first time," says Emily, "exchanging information and ideas.... We learned so much about Dan we'd never known before—how desperately he'd needed our approval. As the oldest of the children, he'd always been made to feel that he had to set an example. No wonder the strain proved too much. And he learned a few things about us, too—that we have our fears and doubts, that our marriage hasn't always been perfect, that Bob and I disagree and argue about all sorts of things in spite of the united front we've always maintained before the children...."

The Colemans feel that they are now better equipped to deal with their younger children. "We're going to be more honest with them and more aware of them as separate individuals. And all we're hoping is that they'll treat us the same way."

The Hamilton Story

The Hamiltons' fifteen-year-old daughter, Carrie, started taking drugs while attending a fashionable private school in Los Angeles. She explains it this way: "I'm compulsive and I'm an extremist and I did have a big ego. I wanted to be a Big Something. If I couldn't be the big wheel, at least I could be the big dope fiend."

Carol Burnett and Joe Hamilton watched helplessly as their daughter slipped into the oblivion of drugs. For two years, during which Carrie was up to two grams of cocaine a day, they tried negotiating, begging, threatening, but their efforts were futile.

At that time, Carol Burnett says, "It didn't dawn on us that we were dealing with a walking chemical. When that dawned on us, we got very strong. From that moment on Carrie's recovery was simply a matter of time."

Carol and Joe give full credit to a drug rehabilitation program in which they placed their daughter. She fought against going, but her parents now saw themselves as dealing, not with a reasonable almost-adult, but with a sick child in need of help. They had reasserted their parental authority at a time when they realized their daughter was incapable of making her own decisions.

Carol Burnett's message to parents is: "Look, if your kid has a brain tumor, you're not going to perform the operation. What makes you think just because you're Mommy and Daddy that you can deal with drug addiction?" And she urges parents not to be afraid of their children. "Don't be afraid they will hate you, because they already do. It's the chemical in them. They don't care about you. All they care about is getting high."

My daughter was in her freshman year at San Francisco State College when I discovered that she was taking LSD. Her experimentation with the drug can probably be ascribed to "the new conformity." In her early teens, she was marked as "different" because of her extreme shyness and bookishness, and in the Connecticut suburb where we lived at the time that was enough to exclude her from the social activities of her peers. It made for a lonely and painful adolescence, and for wild mood swings—from deep depression to an almost feverish gaiety. At college her greatest desire was simply "to belong," and dropping acid, as she saw it, was one way to win the approval of her classmates.

We talked about all this when I flew to San Francisco to confront her with what I knew. The confrontation turned into an encounter session. In her cramped apartment near the college, we talked far into the night, for the first time, dropping out of our Mother-Daughter roles and meeting each other as woman to woman.

But we were not yet ready to move out of our symbiosis and into the transition from Parent/Child to Friend. She was still afraid of what awaited her "out there" and wanted an open-ended option to return to the nest in case it proved too much for her to handle on her own. And I was not prepared to begin surrendering my role as Mother. At the time I had no idea what to put in its place. It took me several more years, and there were many more inner changes, before I discovered what that was.

6
Mating Time

In the parent-child relationship timing is everything. From the moment a child is conceived, the biological clock begins ticking away, its silent alarm set to go off at critical events in the life cycle: birth, puberty, menopause, death. Under normal circumstances the timepieces of parents and children should be fairly well synchronized: As the child is growing from infancy to puberty, the parents are growing from young adulthood to maturity and are finding their biological satisfactions in "generativity." As the children pass through puberty on their way to adulthood, the parents are moving through the midyears toward what has been referred to as "the menopause that refreshes." The equation is still roughly in balance, the young adult child achieving a high level of sexuality at about the time the parents' sexual powers are at their peak. Sometime during the postmenopausal years the sexuality of the parents begins declining, but by this time the children are absorbed with their own parenting, and the pleasure in the new generation compensates the aging parents for the loss of their sexual and reproductive functions.

At least, that's the way the script would be written if biology were the only force at work. But since an infinite number of cultural forces are operating, often at cross-purposes to biology, the parent-child scripts that so many of us are acting out bear little resemblance to the idealized version mentioned above. In the real world, at this time in history, the developing sexuality of our children has in many cases been more of a dilemma than a delight. True, we felt a surge of pride when our daughters began menstruating and our sons ejaculating—("Our little girl is a woman!" "Our little boy is a man!")—but the pride was mixed with apprehension. As parents of adult children we are indelibly stamped as pre-Kinseyan vintage. We may flaunt our sexual freedom, choosing our bed mates as casually as we choose groceries at the supermarket; we may swing high or low and maintain that sex is just fun and games, to be taken no more seriously than a set of tennis; but somewhere, at a subconscious level, lurks a fear of sex as a mysterious power that divides and conquers. In that subbasement of our psyche, we sense that our children's sexuality is the enemy, that our weapons are not equal to the battle, and that somewhere down the road, as our rear-guard action collapses, we will be pushed aside in favor of new attachments in our children's lives.

Sex at the Great Divide

We come smack up against another paradox here: In moving from an era of rigid sexual attitudes to a time of sexual freedom and openness, we are not seeing an easing of sex-related problems between parents and children. On the contrary, this type of problem has been on the increase. Witness the growing number of people who are seeking sexual and marital counseling and who trace their troubles to intergenerational conflicts.

Why hasn't the sexual revolution lived up to its promise of improving our relationships all around? If so many of us who are parents of grown children accept, or at least tolerate, the new morality, as the studies show, why do sex-related tensions set parents and adult children on either side of the Great Divide?

As in the case of drugs and religious cults, those of us who were formed by the ethos of the old values still have embedded in our consciousness some vestiges of the sexual code of an earlier time. The sexual value system that prevailed during our pubescent years was, first of all, as covert as a secret agent's instructions. Sex education took place neither at school nor at home, but in the streets, the playgrounds, and the other hangouts where we met and mingled with our peers after school. We educated each other, trading exaggerations and misinformation in shocked whispers. I have the impression that my brothers picked up what they knew at an earlier age and in a somewhat more factual form than I did. But then, girls were more carefully sheltered from the "facts of life," the theory being, apparently, that what they didn't know wouldn't hurt them. The extent of our ignorance about sex can hardly be imagined today, when children seem to acquire sexual knowledge not long after they are weaned.

"I knew less about sex even after I was married," my friend Paula once told me, "than kids today know when they're in second grade. Would you believe, when I'd been married about two years, I went to a doctor to find out why I couldn't get pregnant, and he asked me a lot of questions. I was so embarrassed, I didn't know where to look. One of the questions was: Do you have orgasms? And I said: Oh no! I'm perfectly healthy. Today, not only does every little fourteen-year-old dollie know all about orgasms, she thinks she has a constitutional right to have them."

Our ignorance about sex was compounded by our acceptance of the reigning myths, which were dutifully disseminated by the movies and the pulp magazines. According to these myths, sex was something men enjoyed, women put up with; no decent man would marry a woman who was not a virgin; the hymen could be ruptured as a result of vigorous exercise, so that, if necessary, tennis or horseback riding could explain the loss of virginity; men needed sexual variety, but women could be satisfied with one sex partner; an illegitimate child was a disgrace; masturbation was dirty and unhealthy, and brought on physical debilitation and possibly irreversible brain damage.

By the time our children were in grade school most of this mythology had been swept away by the gusts of change, and whatever remained was wiped out by the sexual revolution. We overcame our ignorance about sex and are able today to talk knowledgeably about such matters as the libido, the female orgasm, penis envy, foreplay, extramarital intercourse. We learned, thanks to Kinsey, that sexual behavior in America has all along been something very different from what was allowed by the socially accepted code. But this new-found sexual awareness has not only done little to improve relationships between men and women, it has also failed to ease generational tensions relating to the issue of sexuality. We can only conclude that sexual literacy is not enough, or that we have not yet learned to apply it to the most basic human relationships.

Psychoanalyst Anne Steinmann, a specialist in sexual dysfunction, finds a clue to the sexual confusions of both generations in our failure to make a distinction between "sex" and "sexuality." "Sex," by her definition, refers specifically to the physical act of sex. On the other hand, she speaks of sexuality as "the total interaction of a man and woman in every aspect of their living together, with a daily appreciation of their individual sexual, emotional and intellectual drives. . . ." "Sexuality," she adds, "represents a completion—a wholeness and continuity of affection and communication between two people."

"Unfortunately," says Dr. Steinmann, "we have tended in recent years to isolate sex and remove it from the context of sexuality. We have placed undue emphasis on technique so that sex begins to resemble an athletic performance, a matter of training, agility, and prowess. It's not how you feel but how you do it that counts—and what you get out of it for yourself." If both generations are experiencing feelings of guilt and inadequacy, of being losers in the sexual "game," can it be that we are making the mistake of perceiving sex as a game and trying to live up to an arbitrary set of rules and standards?

Asexual Role Players

As long as we remain in the role of Parent and our adult children in the role of Child, there will be a door closing us off from each other with an invisible sign on it marked "Private. Do Not Intrude." Even when parents are comfortable with their own sexuality, they are not comfortable about sharing it with their children. And our adult children, while they may be completely at ease about their own sexuality, display great uneasiness when confronting that of their parents or anyone of their parents' generation.

As parents we contribute to this process of mutual concealment and mystification by hiding our sexuality from our children. One of our greatest terrors is that they might catch us *in flagrante.* We carefully lock the door before making love, to prevent this from happening, and we never refer in any way to our sexual impulses or activities. By shrouding our sex lives in mystery, we believe that we are protecting our parental image as sanctified guardians of the family morals.

In this, many of us succeed all too well, so that not only does our sexuality remain hidden from our children, but our children's sex lives are just as carefully hidden from us. The eighteen-year-old girl who, for two years, kept her mother in ignorance about her abortion, is not a special case. Even parents who feel that they are in close touch with their children admit that they know very little about their children's sexual activities. The withdrawal of the adolescent child that marks the beginning of parent-child noncommunication has its origins almost entirely in the "sexual mystique" that exists between generations. When I remarked on this to a thirty-two-year-old psychologist during one of our early interviews, she showed me part of a letter she had received some years ago from her younger sister, who was seventeen at the time and was suffering the agonies of her first serious love affair:

"I have such a very strange relationship with Mom and Dad. I love them with all my heart and I feel incredibly close to them, yet at the same time there is a vast distance between us. Last Thursday I wanted so much to go to them and say: 'I canceled my hair appointment for this week because I met a very beautiful boy and we went to his place together and he tore me apart with his tenderness and honesty, and I want to make love to him.' But I couldn't say it. This is something they'll never understand. There are so many thousands of facets of love which they just won't acknowledge or accept."

The irony in this, the psychologist said, is that her parents are earthy, sensual people with a broad streak of tolerance and good humor. "But," she added, "I've only been able to see them that way recently, when they began treating me as a separate person. They haven't yet been able to do this with my younger sister, probably because she's the baby of the family. Sometimes, with the youngest, the separation trauma is the most severe and the most difficult to work through successfully."

Sex and Parental Expectations

Relating to each other as asexual beings, parents and children tend to develop mutual expectations in the sex and mating departments that act as emotional levers, raising the level of tension and frustration on both sides. As parents watching our children grow to manhood and womanhood, we allow our fantasies full rein, envisioning for our sons and daughters the sexual and marital fulfillment that has eluded us. But however far our expectations may wander in the realm of fantasy, they are, like our values and beliefs, rooted in generational consciousness. My mother's expectations for me were that I would be a virgin when I married (any other possibility was unthinkable), that there would be a big, splashy wedding at which she, as mother of the bride, would enjoy her transcendent moment of glory, that my new home would be close to hers, and that I would produce a reasonable number of children within a reasonable number of years who would be the comfort and joy of her old age.

As for her picture of the man I was to marry, it was somewhat hazy and unfocused, since she saw him as an unfortunate but necessary appendage to my life—unfortunate because he would remove me physically from her immediate family orbit, but necessary for me to attain the status of marriage. She did, however, have a few specifics. He was to be several things my father was not—that is, steady, faithful, and devout. He should also be a good provider, which my father was only sporadically. He should, of course, be healthy, clean-living, of impeccable moral standards, and good to his mother, if he had one. She took it for granted that he would be good to her, his mother-in-law.

Although my mother's expectations were not fulfilled in every respect, I came fairly close to the mark. Was this because, given her strength and single-mindedness, I could not help acting out her scenario? Possibly. But I think there was something else. The life choices and options available to girls of my generation were fairly limited, so that, whatever our personal expectations, we were not likely to wander too far from the traditional life our parents envisioned for us. The men we dated and later married were drawn from a fairly restricted circle that conformed in most respects to our families' criteria for our mates. Once married, we intended to have children, and most of us expected to be full-time mothers. As for our male contemporaries, their lives may have been less circumscribed, but they, too, with few exceptions, fell back into familiar patterns when the time came for choosing a mate and starting a family. Some of us disappointed our parents by marrying people they did not personally care for, but, after all, the in-law problem was as ancient as marriage and the frictions it caused could be absorbed into the normal pattern of family life. Some of us got divorces, and that was harder for our now aging parents to accept. But by that time divorce was becoming sufficiently commonplace for the adjustment to be made without serious difficulty.

How different it has been for our present generation of parents and the children around whom we wove our hopes and fancies. We, too, expected our children to marry and have families of their own. Our sons, we anticipated, would do some "playing around" before they settled on the girl they wanted to marry. Our daughters—well, they might have an affair or two before they married, virginity no longer being the entrance requirement for holy matrimony. But though our standards for our children's mating behavior have been more relaxed than those of our parents, we have expected or even assumed that our children's lovers and life partners would be "people like us," and that their family life would eventually resemble ours in most respects.

As earlier generations had done, we could have absorbed a normal rate of change in mating rites and patterns. The man I married had been married before and did not have a proper religious divorce, but since he met all my mother's other requirements for a son-in-law, she was able to overlook this single deviation from her code. My brother went farther afield by marrying a woman of another religion, but again, since his wife resembled in most other respects my mother's mental image of a daughter-in-law, this shock was soon cushioned by my mother's basic good sense and dedication to family unity.

But the mating options available to our children have gone far beyond such minor deviations from the social code. Within a few short years traditional sexual attitudes and behaviors have been torn out by the roots, and where once there were a few neat and recognizable growths, there is now a dense and tangled foliage, bearing what to many midlife parents appears to be strange and indigestible fruit. Today, marriage is only one of many life styles available to our children, and sexual arrangements may take any number of forms, according to the needs and desires of the individuals involved.

It seems quaint, even archaic now, to think that

only ten years ago, when she was away at college, my daughter could not bring herself to tell me face to face that she and her boyfriend were living together. She broke the news in a letter, in which she assured me that theirs was no ordinary infatuation, but a love that is "tangible, constant, something that can give a scared, lonely little life the ability to meet the world on whatever terms it must be met." Today, most of the parents I come across whose children are old enough to marry are strongly in favor of premarital cohabitation for their daughters as well as their sons, seeing this arrangement as a more rational expression of sexuality than the repressive standards of our day. A woman in her fifties, recently divorced, told me that she and her husband had married only for sex. "We couldn't have it any other way," she said. "I'm delighted that my daughters are both living with their boyfriends instead of rushing into marriage. Sex is no big deal for them, and if and when they do marry, it will be for other reasons aside from sexual attraction."

Yes, we have come a long way, but for many of us there is still a long way to go before we and our adult children can meet each other as friends who are also sexual beings, with a wide range of needs, appetites, and preferences.

The Homosexual Child

In a time of rapid, constant flux we tend to cling to whatever appears to us as fixed points in a shifting landscape. By the time our children reached adulthood the sexual revolution was in full swing, and in the area of sex and marriage there were few fixed points left to cling to, but most of us persisted in our conviction that one of these remaining fixities was sexual identity.

Even before the child's birth the question of gender is predominant, the most frequent question asked of prospective parents being, Do you want a boy or a girl? The thought apparently never occurs to the questioners or the expectant parents that the child might turn out to be neither clearly one nor the other. From the moment of birth we begin reinforcing the child's gender—pink for girls, blue for boys—and this continues through the growing-up years by means of repeated admonitions that "boys don't do this, girls don't do that," right on through high school and college, in which boys have until recently been steered toward science and technology, girls toward the liberal arts.

The belief that "men are men, women are women," and all others are "queers" is part of the American creed, a byproduct of the frontier ethic. Despite the gay liberation movement and the general relaxation of attitudes toward sexual deviation, it is still a severe blow to most parents whose consciousness bears the imprint of traditional folkways to discover that a son is a homosexual or a daughter a lesbian.

The subject of sexual preference has been taboo for such a long time that it is still, even in these sexually enlightened times, surrounded by an astonishing amount of ignorance and misinformation. Stereotypes of mincing, effeminate males and muscular, husky-voiced females have obscured our view of homosexual behavior in the real world. The continuing prejudice against homosexuals, particularly in high-status professions and occupations, deepens parental despair when a son or daughter is revealed as having homosexual tendencies. That there are homosexuals and lesbians leading normal, satisfying lives is something that is inconceivable to the larger part of heterosexual society. Surveys conducted during the seventies by CBS-TV and the Institute for Sex Research at Indiana University, both based upon a large representative sample of Americans, found that two-thirds regarded homosexuality as "very obscene and vulgar," and almost one half feared homosexuality as "a corruption that can cause the downfall of civilization."

Because of this widespread abhorrence, adult children who are homosexuals often prefer to make a complete break from their parents rather than admit their sexual preference. There are parents whose children have been lost to them—"as if he were dead," said one father of his only son—as a consequence of child and parent being unable to confront the subject of the child's sexuality.

What, then, can parents do if they want to continue their connection with an adult child who is leading a homosexual life? I found several parents who have been able to maintain the tie in varying degrees. In Boulder, Colorado, I talked with a fifty-year-old mother of five grown children who told me how she changed the relationship with her homosexual son, Freddie:

"I'm not sure just when I began suspecting that Freddie was a homosexual. It was sometime during the teen years, and I suppose the idea came into my head when I noticed that he wasn't interested in doing the kinds of things boys did. He had no interest in football or athletics generally, or in girls. He was different in many ways. But we never talked about it. Freddie has always been a very private person . . . maybe that's because of his homosexuality. I respected that privacy and I would never violate it or embarrass him in any way. I'd always had such a marvelous relationship with Freddie. Had there been any conflict, if I'd thought he was in any trouble or unhappy, I might have brought it up. But there was none of that. He conducted his life in such a satisfactory way that there was no reason for me to intrude.

"By the time he had graduated from college I had no doubt about his homosexuality—but somehow I was able to make the adjustment to that, maybe because I'd never had any prejudice against homosexuals. The trauma for me was that, because Freddie wasn't able to talk to me about it, our relationship was becoming strained. His sense of privacy was turning into secretiveness. When he moved to Denver, I knew he was living with a young man. I found out from a friend who visited him; Freddie never told me. In fact, by this time we'd grown so far apart, there was almost no contact between us.

"I realized that if we were ever going to have a relationship again, we would have to talk about his homosexuality. And so I came to a decision. I knew I would have to be the initiator, that it was easier for me to let him know I knew than for him to tell me. I had a feeling that there'd been several times in the past when he'd been on the verge of telling me and had drawn back. . . .

"What made it difficult for me was that he was twenty-six now; he was a man, he could do as he pleased. If he wanted to cut me out of his life, that was a choice he could make. Maybe this is the way it was going to be with us from now on. How did I know? I only knew that it didn't feel right, to me. So I took a chance. I sent him a very brief note, nine words: 'I know you're gay. I love you very much.'

"He came to Boulder the next weekend, stayed at a motel, but visited with us at the house, had Sunday dinner with us for the first time in over a year. And after the first few awkward moments I knew it was going to be all right. He needed to have it brought out. He said to me, 'I thought you knew, but I wasn't sure.' And then we talked—oh, on and on— it was like opening the floodgates. He told me about his problems, about how desperately unhappy he'd been at times, how he wasn't even sure he was a homosexual, that someday he might even be attracted to a girl, might get married. I didn't know whether he was still trying to ease something in himself or in me. You know, I've heard about and read about parents for whom this thing is a terrible trauma, but I can tell you, from my experience, it's much worse for the young man or woman who's going through it. They need all the support and friendship and understanding you can give them.

"It's about a year and a half since Freddie and I had our confrontation, and it's only now that he's beginning to believe that his homosexuality doesn't bother me at all. It took a little longer for his father to accept it, but now that's okay too. Which sort of surprised me, because my husband is not all that tolerant ... but because he cares so much about his son, he was able to take him as he is. The only thing that concerns us is Freddie's suffering—it's a damn cruel world out there, and it's painful for someone as vulnerable as Freddie to try to cope with it. But he's getting a lot of strength from us, now that he's comfortable with us and knows that we're comfortable with him."

Accepting a child's homosexuality in order to maintain the relationship often accelerates the process of disconnecting as parent and reconnecting as friend. In our role as parents, our children's sexuality becomes instrumental—a means of achieving the continuity we prize by replicating our sexual and familial patterns. At the gut level we want our children to mate with "people like us"; we want our grandchildren to carry our genes. We are unhappy about sexual deviation in our children, not only because of the social opprobrium but also because the homosexual child represents a genetic dead end. In friendship, however, there is no vested interest in biological continuity. Nor are we particularly concerned with the sexual preferences of our friends, which, we would surely insist, are their own business. The transference of this tolerant attitude to the homosexual child is all that is required to preserve and strengthen the parent-child relationship, and provide the child who is "different" with much-needed moral support.

Marriage As Long As You Dig It

In the late 1960s *Time* magazine described the nuptials of a young couple as follows: "The bride wore nothing. Neither did the groom, nor, for that matter, the officiating cleric, a minister of the religious-diploma mill known as the Universal Life Church, Inc. The ceremony was as stark as the apparel. Dropping a stick before the couple, the pastor pronounced the legal essentials in mod vernacular: 'You're married as long as you dig it.' " How, I wonder, did the parents—assuming they were present and fully clothed—feel about this ceremony?

The rites of marriage in recent years appear to be edging back toward the more traditional forms, but marriage itself no longer resembles the earlier model that served us and generations before us. The idea that marriage is forever is probably gone forever, and the words "till death do us part" have become something of a joke. In a panel discussion at Princeton University, the following was suggested as a model of the various relationships that people can develop in the course of their lives: first, living alone for a time after leaving the parental home; then living with someone of the opposite sex; this to be followed by marriage, not necessarily to one's former live-in partner; following the dissolution of this marriage, moving on to sharing a home with a friend of the same sex; afterwards, a second marriage in which the partners spend only part of their time together; and, finally, in the later years, when one is alone again, living as part of a group in some type of communal arrangement.[1]

Unlike the Princeton model, the social consensus on the subject of mating during my youthful years was pretty much an either-or proposition. If you were female, you were either married by the early to midtwenties or there were the following possibilities: You were so unattractive, no one would marry you; you were a lesbian; you were both.

If you were male and not married by the time

[1]See Leslie Aldridge Westoff, "Two-Time Winners," *New York Times Magazine* (August 10, 1975).

you were thirty or thereabouts, you were either a homosexual or a mamma's boy, or both. Adults were
expected to arrange themselves in pairs and go
through life two by two, like the animals in the ark.
There was nothing comparable to today's "swinging
single." Being single was considered an unfortunate
condition, situated somewhere between a physical
handicap and a social disease.

A lifelong marriage was viewed as the only desirable relationship between a man and a woman. We
recognized the possibility of divorce (there had been
one or two in the family that no one talked about),
but we regarded it as a tragedy to be avoided at all
costs. And the costs could be considerable, going as
high at times as the denial of love and sexual fulfillment for the better part of a lifetime. Loveless, even
desperately unhappy marriages were preserved "for
the sake of the children," to avoid a public admission
of failure, for economic reasons—for all kinds of reasons having nothing to do with the needs of the two
people immediately involved.

I offer two exhibits as illustrations of the generation gap in the marriage-and-divorce department.
Exhibit A is a scrap of dialogue between a mother
and her married daughter, aged fifty-three and twenty-eight respectively. The daughter, married for five
years and with a three-year-old child, is contemplat-
ing divorce and is discussing her difficulties with her
mother.

DAUGHTER: We function well together, we have
a business relationship, but at night, when he wants
to make love to me, I just can't.

MOTHER: Are you saying you have (*hesitantly,
with some embarrassment*) sex problems?

DAUGHTER: You don't go to bed with your business partner, do you? I put up with it at times to avoid a long serious discussion in bed.

MOTHER: And this is so important to you—this sex business?

DAUGHTER: It's hard to explain; it's all feelings. I guess you and Dad never had any problems in bed.

MOTHER: We didn't talk about these things.

DAUGHTER: I have to talk about it. I can't keep it bottled up any longer. Look—it's not just sex. It's that—the fun has gone out of it. He's always so intense with me, so serious. I wish he were more of a pal.

MOTHER: I think you're expecting too much out of marriage. You have a child now; you can't be thinking only of yourself. You have to learn to put up with things—for the sake of your child.

DAUGHTER: But if I'm unhappy, if I'm not good for myself, how can I be good for my child?

Exhibit B is a brief excerpt from a letter sent by a father to his married son. The son's marriage of eight years has produced two children, and now a divorce is imminent. The letter concludes as follows:

"If you both find, after repeated and earnest efforts, that for whatever reasons your lives do not fit together, that one or both of you cannot together achieve that minimum of happiness to which human beings feel they are entitled, then by all means separate and start all over again in your own separate ways. But such a step, especially when there are two other human beings involved, needs very careful and patient exploration, because it's so much more difficult to find happiness and fulfillment through negation than through affirmation."

In both exhibits the parents are acting out the parental role: The needs of the daughter and the son and of their spouses as individuals are placed in the larger context of marriage and family. The "old values" of self-denial and deferred gratification are expressed by the parents as against the "new values," which emphasize the all-powerful "I" and its needs, and which insist on the right to happiness *now*—not at some time in the hazy, unpredictable future.

Which generation has the sounder, more reasonable approach? Neither—and both. Attempting to impose our ideas of sex and marriage on our adult children would be futile and unproductive, as would be their attempt to impose theirs on us. In the generational dialectic, keeping the communication open and flowing freely back and forth makes it possible for us to maintain our mutual sympathy and understanding, which are the basis for any sustained relationship. Mating time is when the parent-child connection should be reinforced in every possible way, because, as most parents who become parents-in-law can testify, the problems that arise when our children marry put the relationship with them to its severest test.

In-Laws as Outlaws

Has there ever been a more uncomfortable role than that of mother-in-law? The butt of an endless stream of jokes, she is caricatured in comic strips, sitcoms, and other pop media. According to folk wisdom, the daughter's husband resents his mother-in-law because she is an ever-present reminder of what his attractive young wife will be one day. Fathers-in-

law have somehow escaped this universal opprobrium; I don't recall ever hearing a father-in-law joke.
This may be because fathers have been regarded as
having a lesser influence in family matters, and perhaps also because in our society an older man is not
as pitiable an object as an older woman. But the father-in-law role, perhaps because of its very insignifi-
cance, is not exactly an enviable one to be thrust into
either.

When our children marry, we must confront the
fact that it creates a major shift in our connection
with them. Our son or daughter, having formed a
new bond, is now connected to another person, who
is, for all practical purposes, replacing the parent.
What stance can the parent take toward a once-sin-
gle being who has now become a twosome? And
what exactly is the nature of our relationship to the
Other Person?

We tell ourselves that we are delighted to see
the children married and self-sufficient. And for a
part of us this is true. But there's another part that
is secretly pleased when the marriage runs into problems and our son or daughter seeks us out for advice. And this is the dangerous part of us—the
possessive parent longing to be once again the center
of the child's universe, the dispenser of love and comfort. "After all, he/she still needs me," says that in-
sidious little interior voice. And though our son or
daughter may have come to us looking for the kind
of help that can be had only from a close friend, we
respond from the position of parent, hoping that we
can still mold our child to conform to our values and
expectations.

It is that part of us that sees the son- (or daugh-
ter-) in-law as an interloper, a thief in the night who

has stolen our child away. And we strongly suspect that this "outsider" sees us in an equally unfavorable light. "My daughter-in-law hates me," a handsome sixty-year-old woman told me. "She considers me a competitor for my son's affections. But she has nothing to worry about—" This was said with some bitterness—"My son, with whom I once had a warm and loving relationship, has made it clear that she's the one, and I don't even figure in his scheme of things. When I told that to my shrink, he said, 'It's entirely possible to love one's wife and one's mother simultaneously; the two loves are not mutually exclusive!' But apparently it's not possible for my son."

The same woman remarked on another occasion that her daughter-in-law always keeps her firmly fixed in the mother-in-law role. "When she introduces me, it's always as Robert's mother. I keep telling myself that next time I won't let her get away with it. I rehearse what I'm going to say: 'I have my own name . . . and I was a person before Robert existed.' But somehow, when the moment comes, I always lose my courage."

"As an in-law I feel like an outlaw," said a divorced professor, father of three married sons. "I'm never sure whether I'm supposed to act like a surrogate father to my daughters-in-law—or should I adopt a flirtatious tone, entirely in fun, of course? It's really quite an awkward situation."

It can become even more awkward when the young couple divorces. The parents-in-law feel the full brunt of the split-up, especially when there are children who are shuttled between the parents, or on special family occasions. A friend whom I lunch with occasionally described a Passover dinner she attended at what used to be the home of her son and daughter-in-law, shortly after her son moved out and divorce proceedings were under way. "I went there only because Steve insisted. He said it was for the sake of the children. And there she was, her high-ness, presiding over the dinner table, displaying the gifts I'd given her over the years—the Spode china, the silver tray, the pewter candlesticks that belonged to my mother.... Her boss sat on one side of her and, on the other side, her boyfriend, who was now sleeping in Steve's bed.

"Throughout the dinner she kept making dispar-aging remarks about Steve: 'Men are such infants,' 'I never should have married or had children,' and so on. I was speechless; I couldn't utter a sound. I left early, went home, and threw up."

Why is the parent-in-law role so uncomfortable? The answer is not difficult to find. In our society it has become superfluous and obsolete, a vestige of tribalism and the extended family, of a time when the members of the older generation monopolized the financial power in the family and continued to rule the roost until their death. Gerontocracy still ex-ists in some Oriental societies, but with few excep-tions, rule by elders does not fit in with the realities of our highly developed technological society. The in-law role should be marked for extinction. By the time a son or daughter marries, the parent should have completed the process of transformation from parent to friend. As an ex-parent you cannot be a parent-in-law. Your attitude toward your son-in-law or daugh-ter-in-law is the same as toward your son or daughter: You are a close and caring friend to both.

True, you have a more intimate knowledge of your own child than of your child-in-law, but this need not distort your vision or warp your reasoning powers. From the position of friendship you should be able to view the young couple as two individuals, each with a separate, complex set of needs, emotions, desires, and both engaged in an effort to accomplish a delicate and very difficult feat: the merging of their love while retaining their separate identities.

Establishing yourself as a fair-minded and impartial friend makes it possible for you to function effectively as a mediator—a role you will be called upon to perform from time to time. As a parent or parent-in-law you are hampered in your ability to act as arbitrator in the children's disputes by the tendency to fall back into stereotyped behavior. You will either automatically take up the cause of your own child ("Poor baby, I can imagine what you've been going through. . . . Of course, I always knew he/she was a supreme egotist.") or, if you always criticized your child, your response will most likely follow the same pattern ("You were always impulsive and emotionally unstable. You could never keep a job or stick to a commitment. It doesn't surprise me that you can't make a success of your marriage.")

When my daughter was having some painful problems in her marriage, she wrote to me, "not as a little girl unable to look after herself but as a grown woman to one of her closest friends, the friend who knows her the most thoroughly of all her friends." I phoned her to say I was taking the next flight to London and that I wanted to be sure my son-in-law would be there too. In the days that followed we had many long talks—a few one-to-one, others as a threesome.

It was like letting out the steam in a pressure cooker, but it soon became clear to me that they needed more professional counseling than I could give them. Soon after, they were fortunate enough to find a wise and skillful counselor, who helped them put their marriage back together again. But though my part in the ultimate reconciliation was limited, I felt that during this period the three of us had reaffirmed our friendship and strengthened our ties of trust and affection.

Why Have Children?

One of the conflict areas between parents and children today is the children's decision not to have children. An assumption that went virtually unchallenged for my generation and those preceding us was that the purpose of marriage was to produce children. With the technology of birth control at the time either very primitive or nonexistent, there was very little choice in the matter. A married couple who, in due time, failed to have a child were, like single people, objects of pity, and the woman was generally considered to be responsible for this biological catastrophe.

For today's young marrieds the situation in regard to having children has changed so drastically that it seems as if the two generations must be living in different time warps. Today the decision to have children is exactly that—a decision, a conscious choice. And the woman's movement has combined with the inflationary economy to make that choice, increasingly, a negative one.

The number of female college graduates choosing not to have children has more than doubled in less than ten years, according to a study by a midwestern college. The study concludes that these are well-adjusted women, who are willing to live their lives without taking on the role of parent. Most of them see themselves as reaching higher levels in their professions than women did before and are more likely to choose careers that have been traditionally dominated by men, such as medicine, law, computer science, engineering.

For parents, it often comes as a blow to have a married daughter or son announce, "We've decided we're not going to have children." One of the fathers I interviewed said: "I'm proud of my daughter's success. She's a lawyer, with a good practice. And her husband is a plastic surgeon, one of the best. They've been married ten years—my daughter's almost forty—and they're not going to have children, they're definite about that. We used to argue about it all the time, but no more. It's no use. It makes me feel as though there's nothing to look forward to. How can people be so selfish? Don't my wife and I have a right to be grandparents?"

I was tempted to remind him that this was not one of his inalienable rights, but as a grandmother I can empathize with his sense of loss and disappointment. The birth of my granddaughter was, for me, a peak experience. I felt that I now owned a piece of the future, that I was no longer merely a transient on earth, but rather a permanent resident in the universal scheme.

In our generational value system, continuity—the future—looms large. But for a generation that has grown up under the threat of thermonuclear war, the future and the idea of continuity have no reality. When the only time dimension that matters is the present, the desire for children lessens in intensity. As for the charge of self-centeredness that parents sometimes level at their childless children, the comeback "Why *not* be self-centered?" reflects the ethos of young adults who are searching for something outside of themselves to believe in and hand on to future generations.

As a parent you resent being cut off from the future. You had counted on having grandchildren to fill the empty spaces in your later years, and you manage to make your children feel guilty about their dereliction. But as an ex-parent you can appreciate your children, and their mates, for themselves, and not as vehicles for your aspiration to biological immortality. If grandparenting is important to you, there are children in hospitals, orphanages, or right in your neighborhood who could use a proxy grandparent. And you can fill those empty spaces with interests and activities of your own and free yourself from dependence on or resentment of the life your married children have chosen.

Interracial Mating

Can it be that the urge to live on in our children, to perpetuate something of our personal identity, is also at the source of the parent-child problems that are generated by interracial mating? This idea seems to offer at least a partial explanation for the strong negative feelings that surge up in parents when their child chooses a mate from a different racial stock. We are dealing here, after all, with a generation of parents who are, for the most part, liberal and progressive in their thinking. Some of them were in the forefront of the civil rights movement and, more recently, of the drive to integrate schools. Most of them would reject vigorously the notion that there is any bigotry in their makeup.

And yet, when the issue is a son's or daughter's sexual and marital relationships, the reactions of many parents, both white and nonwhite, range from mild uneasiness to strong disapproval. The responses that come forth with the greatest frequency include: "Marriage is difficult enough when both are from the same background. Why add on extra problems?" "I'm not a racist, but I am religious, and I don't think God meant for the races to mix." "People in a racially mixed marriage have to buck a society that, like it or not, still has a lot of prejudices." "What about the children? It's hardest on the children." And here and there a mother or father will admit, "I can't help it—I just can't face the idea of grandchildren who are not my color."

Where such feelings prevail, it often means the deterioration and, ultimately, the breaking of the parent-child connection if the child chooses a sex partner of another race. Because of the history of black-white relations in America, white middle-class parents appear to have more negative feelings toward blacks than toward Orientals. But this can't be simply dismissed as racism; powerful psychological and cultural forces are at work, along with the biological motivations. As I delved further into this theme, I found the variations and permutations multiplying.

There is, for example, Julia, a slim, vibrant black woman with a successful law practice who is married to Herbert, a Jewish physician. It is the second marriage for both, and both have children whose ages range from the early teens to the early twenties. Although they had been together for five years before marrying and felt that they had worked out most of their problems, there have been some bumps along the road. "Herbert's mother could not accept a black daughter-in-law," Julia says. "She wouldn't come to our house or have us over to hers. Herbert and I agreed that he shouldn't visit her without me, so we dealt with that one by meeting her on neutral ground—at a hotel. I've never believed in forcing relationships. I knew where Herbert's mother was coming from, and I didn't want him to suffer. When you love someone, you want to spare him as much pain as possible. And you know, people can change if you give them time. Just recently my mother-in-law invited us to her house for the first time, and when we arrived, you know what she did? She gave me a lovely old brooch that had belonged to her mother. I can imagine what it meant to her to do that, and I'm sure she realizes what it meant to me."

How about the children? I wondered. Julia said: "Here again we've been careful not to force anything. Herbert doesn't try to be a father to my children, I don't try to be a mother to his. Maybe those relationships will develop in time, maybe they won't. Meanwhile, we're paying attention to ritual and tradition because that's how you get cohesion and continuity in a family. But since our rituals and traditions differ, we're not imposing either mine or his; we're developing our own rituals and traditions—we celebrate our own special occasions in a special way. I think that's what families have to do today—invent their own rituals and traditions to replace those that don't work anymore."

I came across several sets of white parents who were unable to reconcile themselves to their children's interracial unions. In one case the parents as-

sured me: "Our daughter has done this to get back
at us, because we've never gotten along, and she'd
stop at nothing to spit in our faces." And there was
a worn, anxious-looking black mother who said, in regard to her twenty-four-year-old daughter, "I won't
have anything to do with her till she breaks up with
that white man she's living with. He's got nowhere
near her brains and education, and yet she lets him
get away with treating her like dirt."

The White Princess

I was particularly struck by the experience of
Bob and Kitty Ferguson, whom I met while visiting
friends in northern California and who referred to
their twenty-five-year-old daughter, Angela, as "the
white princess." Their daughter was then living with
her third black lover and had gravitated toward
blacks ever since her early teens when she began being attracted to men. "It's her need to feel superior,"
Bob Ferguson said, and his wife nodded in agreement. "But the ironical thing," he went on, "is that
the black men she gets involved with don't cater to
that self-image she has; they're always putting her
down, tearing down her self-esteem. And you don't
have to be a psychologist to realize that Angie's need
to feel superior comes out of a sense of terrible insecurity."

I asked how this had affected their relationship
with their daughter. "At one point it almost finished
us," Bob Ferguson said.

"You have to understand," Kitty Ferguson
quickly added, "that it never meant a thing to us that
her boyfriends were black. It's the kind of human be-

ings they were that bothered us, and the way they treated Angie. Her first boyfriend broke up with her because he told her she wasn't living up to his ideal of what a woman should be. After that she got involved with a black man who was much older than she was, and who'd been married and divorced; he's an industrial designer, a really bright man, and there were many things about him Bob and I liked very much. But it was the same old pattern—he was always humiliating her. After they'd gone around together for a while, they decided to get married; as we expected, the marriage lasted about a year and then they were divorced.

"Through all of this we were supportive; we wanted Angie to know that whenever she needed us, we were there. There was none of this 'Didn't we tell you so?' business——"

"I had a talk with her after the divorce," Bob Ferguson interjected. "I asked her why she was attracted only to black men. She said, 'I prefer black people.' I said, 'That's the epitome of racism; that's just as bad as saying, "I prefer white people." People are people, whatever their color.' But I couldn't get through to her."

"Soon after the divorce," Kitty went on, "she came home and said she was in love again, this time with a really beautiful black man, and she wanted to bring him home to meet the family. When she told me his name, I recognized him as a man I wouldn't have in my house. He'd been in trouble with the law several times, and I knew enough about him to realize I didn't want any part of him. Again, it had nothing to do with his being black. I'd have felt the same way whatever his color.

"When I told Angie how I felt, she became very

angry, and we had one of the worst flare-ups of our lives. She left in a rage and I went upstairs and took a tranquilizer. A week or two later, as I was driving home from the office, I saw her standing on the corner waiting for a bus—and I drove right past her."

"That's not the way we usually do things in our family," Bob Ferguson said. "We're tight-knit, and we don't like to paint ourselves into a corner."

"I don't believe in severing relationships with children," Kitty said. "Whatever happens, we need each other. So my behavior with Angie didn't feel good to me. But I didn't know how to handle it. My emotions were all mixed up—I felt guilty but also angry; I'd go from berating myself to mentally dumping on Angie. Damn her! I'd hear myself thinking, why is she doing this to us? And then the guilt would come over me and I'd remember how, when she was all of twelve years old, she once stood up to me and said, 'I want you to treat me like a person, not a child.'

"Finally, it was Angie who brought things to a head. She dropped in at the office one morning and said she wanted to talk to me. So we went for a walk, and she started right off at a high pitch: 'I don't get it,' she said. 'You're so fucking understanding about everyone, why can't you understand me? What right do you have to approve or disapprove of my friends?' And she went on and on like that till I guess it was out of her system, at which point, I took her in my arms and said, 'You're right. I shouldn't have said what I did and I'm sorry. You have your own life to lead, and I shouldn't be judgmental. If you'll forgive me, I'll do my best from now on to treat you like a person, not a child.' She gave me a hug and I could see that she was struggling to keep back the tears. We didn't say anything for a while, and then I said: 'It works both ways. I want you to treat me like a person, too. I have a right not to associate with people I don't want to associate with, even if they're your friends, and I have a right not to have them at my home.' She was able to accept that from me, and we left each other on good terms."

I asked how things had turned out for Angie, and Kitty said: "She's in Michigan now, living with this man and his family, and she's planning to have a baby with him. And I've been able to adjust to that. I can remember years ago telling Angie and the younger girls, 'Remember, if you get pregnant, it's a lifetime responsibility. Be sure you truly love the father of your child, because it's just not a passing thing; it's forever.' Well, Angie has taught me there's no such thing as forever. It was a painful lesson, but I'm glad I learned it."

When I think about the Fergusons and their "white princess," I wonder what, if anything, their daughter learned from her experience. She must, at the very least, have found that when you demand friendship from a parent, there must be a fair exchange. It may seem obvious to state that parents have as much right to their values as their adult children have to theirs. But obvious or not, many parents of today's young adults feel that, when it comes to the crunch, their values must yield to their children's. With ideas and attitudes being scrapped as rapidly as they are in our time, people in midlife, feeling challenged by a rising generation, are easily led to believe that their value system is out of date and should be consigned to mothballs. They make the mistake of assuming that they must give up their own deeply held beliefs in order to be accepted as a friend and confidant by their children. But what we ask of our friends is honesty and integrity, not a carbon copy of our ideas. What I am particularly impressed with in the Ferguson story is the ability of Angie's parents to view people as individuals rather than as members of a racial group, whereas Angie's behavior, while it may also involve some psychological hang-ups, reflects what her father refers to as "reverse racism," which members of minority groups are usually quick to recognize. A black friend of mine once said, "We don't want to be all wrapped up in virtue. We want the right to be as big sons of bitches as anyone else." Or, to put it another way, the right to be fully human.

It's a right that has yet to be universally recognized, but we are slowly and painfully inching in that direction; and from the time of our generation to that of our adult children there have been some notable changes for the better in relationships between the races. For this development my generation of white middle-class parents can take very little credit. Though many of us considered ourselves free from any taint of prejudice, gave generously to the NAACP, and hailed the Supreme Court decision striking down the "separate but equal" provision for schools, we were also in the vanguard of the postwar flight to the suburbs that provided our children with an environment populated almost exclusively by "people like us."

Oh, we had our euphemisms: "good schools," "fresh air," "safe neighborhoods," "congenial neighbors," "real estate values." And I honestly think we were not aware, in our Cape Cod cottages and early American saltboxes, of how we were shortchanging the American ethic; nor am I suggesting that we should now beat our breasts and utter cries of "Mea culpa." We were acting out the drama of our time, as our children have been acting out the drama of theirs. Our drama was the defeat of the Nazis and the containment of Communism, with the civil rights movement as a sideshow. Theirs has been the extending of equal rights to minorities and to women, with Vietnam as a tragic counterpoint.

But considering the double messages that our children were getting during their formative years, it is not surprising that racism hasn't entirely disappeared among the young and that here and there an Angie Ferguson loses her balance, reacting—or overreacting—against the historic treatment of blacks and other minorities. What *is* surprising—and reassuring—is that so many young adults are interacting with each other as human beings rather than as racial stereotypes, that they have been able to transcend the past and put themselves in touch with the future. Because if we can look far enough down the road with clear, unbiased eyes, we should be able to see that we are moving toward a multiracial society, that the world is becoming internationalized, and that the survival of our children's children may very well depend upon their ability to relate in positive ways to people of various racial, ethnic, and cultural backgrounds.

Sex and the Single Parent

The discomfort that parents and children experience with each other's sexuality is becoming accentuated on the children's side as an increasing number of single parents appear on the scene. The breakup of long-established marriages (the divorce rate in marriages of over twenty years is growing rapidly) is creating a new set of tensions and conflicts between the adult child and the midlife parent who are still tied up in the trappings of the parent-child connection.

As parents we have been so effectively desexualized that it is almost impossible for our children to imagine us in the act of having sex. I still remember how horrified I was when the thought struck me with the force of a head-on collision that my parents had—must have—"done it." Afterward, as I approached adolescence, I resolutely pushed the idea out of my head, privately nourishing the belief that, however others may have come into the world, *I* (and my brothers, too, of course) were products of an immaculate conception, a very special one that did not involve the deity. Eventually it became possible for me to accept my father's sexuality; in fact, in view of the circumstances, it was hardly possible to deny it. But my mother? Never!

The child's fantasizing rarely takes into account the mother's real personality or actual life circumstances. At a discussion following a lecture on human sexuality, a middle-aged woman in the audience said: "My mother was a liberated woman before the expression was invented. She wore pants when that was considered very avant-garde, smoked a corncob pipe, and wrote articles about free love. Still, I could never bear to think of her as having sex."

A psychiatrist tells me that he has come across children who were fully aware that their mothers earned their living as whores, but were able to section off that part of their mothers' lives as being due to economic necessity and continue to think of them in asexual terms. This is a schizophrenic exercise that takes its psychic toll, to be sure, but not so different, perhaps, from an ardent environmentalist rationalizing his father's employment in a polluting industrial plant that provides the only jobs in town: "He has to earn a living, doesn't he?"

As co-conspirators with their adult children in this desexualizing process, single parents have become highly skilled in the use of euphemisms: It is "my friend," "my companion," "someone with whom I'm having a meaningful relationship," but never "my lover." Women as single parents are especially circumspect with their children, in behavior as well as language. There's a message that comes through again and again from single mothers with grown children, particularly if the children are still living at home:

"I feel I have to be a role model for my children. I don't want them to think of me as a sex symbol; they wouldn't have any respect for me if they thought of me that way."

Single mothers are careful to arrange their lives so as to shield the children from the fact that Mother is sleeping with a man. Even when the children are living away from home, the caution is taken. A widow in her early fifties said: "I never allow a man I'm having an affair with to stay overnight. Suppose my married daughter stopped in for coffee in the morning or to drop off my granddaughter, as she often does—and there I am in bed with a man? How could I ever face her again?"

The child's aversion to the thought of a stranger intruding into the parent's life is most acute in the case of the mother-son relationship. When the parents are divorced, the oedipal bond between mother and son is often tightened as the son slips into the role of the absent father. Seeing the mother as lonely and, perhaps, naive, he becomes her guide and mentor, advising her on financial and other family matters. A family counselor who has seen this type of mother-son relationship, in which the mother consults her adolescent son on such matters as whether she should increase the insurance, sell the house, buy a new car or repair the old one, remarked to me: "The kid never before made any decision except where to spend his vacation—and he didn't do that too successfully—and now here he is, in a position of responsibility and power."

The counselor continued: "One day, along comes this guy out of nowhere and moves in on Mamma's life, and all of a sudden he's the one she's looking to for advice and guidance. The son resents having to yield his influential position. Plus, there are financial considerations. The mother may have property, may have a good income, from which she was subsidizing the children. What if this man in her life changes all of that? What if she marries him and he comes in for a hefty share of the inheritance?

"If, in addition, the mother has been playing on the son's sexuality, as many single mothers do, then any man who enters the mother's life is seen as a rival for her affections, and resentment is compounded with jealousy." According to this counselor, a son may take a certain macho pride in his father's "screwing around," but he is repelled at the thought of his mother doing it.

Not that the father as a single parent leads a problem-free existence when he tries to meld his sex life with his parental role. A divorced father who had been living as a swinging bachelor in New York made this discovery when his twenty-two-year-old daughter, whom he had not seen for six years, came to visit him from England, where she had been living with her mother. Suddenly, the father's apartment was declared off limits to the half-dozen or so women who had been taking turns sharing his bed. "I couldn't have that sort of thing going on," said the father flatly. "Not while my little girl was with me."

The single parent's dating and mating options come down to these: (1) go on pretending to be asexual, denying your normal needs and desires, or gratifying them in guilty, furtive ways; (2) be willing to relinquish your parental role, encouraging your adult children to surrender their filial position so that parent and child can confront each other openly and honestly as sexual beings.

Choosing the first option is one way of maintaining the parent-child connection, but since it rests on a false basis, it will have to be shored up constantly through various forms of game playing. Ultimately, this fraudulent exercise drains away much of the vitality and richness that make up a healthy relationship, leaving only the sterile husk of ritualized interactions.

The second option offers a better chance for sustaining the relationship over the long haul, but it is the more difficult course, involving as it does the inner changes of disconnecting and reconnecting that involve deeply held values and the sense of personal identity. It is not easy to emerge from the chrysalis of parenthood—that snug and well-defined enclosure—and find yourself exposed to new demands, without the support of established patterns of behavior. If you have cooperated with your children in developing an image of yourself as a prim, morally upright, asexual parent, it will take some doing before you are able to present yourself as a sexually active human being with normal appetites and some "lovers" among all those "friends," "companions," or "meaningful relationships" of yours. But once you have made the transition, your life as a single parent will become open to new possibilities, and you may be able to bring together into a coherent whole the two worlds you were so careful to keep apart.

7
Money Matters

As a source of conflict and confusion between parents and their adult children, money often heads the list, taking precedence even over sex. Parents can reconcile themselves to a child's sexual life style, which may be incompatible with theirs, since this usually requires no decision or action on their part. However, it can be more difficult for them to divorce themselves from the economic side of their children's lives. The problem of money in families is stubborn and persistent and continues to exert its power, in the form of inheritance, even after the death of the parents.

In many families money is discussed less openly than sex. "I learned about my father's impotence and my mother's sexual repressions by the time I was in college," said a thirty-year-old engineer, "but to this day I'm not really clear about our family finances. I have no idea what my father earned in his used-car business and my mother never knew, either.

He gave us our allowances, and that was that. Money was something we never talked about."

The veil of silence that is drawn over the topic of money serves as a cover for the anxiety and ambivalence in which family finances become enveloped, particularly in middle-income families. Among low-income families, the attitude toward money is clear and straightforward: There is simply not enough of it, and parents and children are united in their awareness of this central, overriding fact. Among the very rich there is more ambiguity, but, again, parents and children are all aware of the family's great wealth, and the privileges and responsibilities that accompany it. We can safely assume that the children of John D. Rockefeller were not deceived by their father's parsimony. Though he kept them on short rations ("What do you think we are—Vanderbilt?" he would demand when his children asked for things he considered extravagant), they could hardly have had any doubt about what it meant, in terms of wealth and power, to be a Rockefeller.

For middle-income families there are no such certainties to cling to. In that great, sprawling economic middle, in which the majority of Americans live, there is a precarious quality about money, a sense that it is subject to shifting forces—inflation, oil prices, employment opportunities, the vagaries of the stock market—over which human beings have no control. Those of us old enough to have adult children carry memories of bread lines and soup kitchens. Money, we believe in our hearts, is not to be trusted, and we propitiate it like a fickle god who controls our destinies. We pay homage to Mammon in a thousand ways, but, perhaps out of some primordial fear of this unpredictable deity, we prefer to keep this part of our lives in the shadows.

As the first generation of affluent parents, we have been caught in a bind—between the opportunities and the dangers that our comfortable finances have offered to our children. The opportunities route led us through a Proustian recapturing of lost time as we attempted to lavish upon our children all that we and our parents were denied in our and their youth. For many of us, this experience was accompanied by an uneasy feeling that we were weakening our children's moral fiber and turning them into financial cripples who would be unable to stand on their own feet in a tough, competitive economy. Some of us succumbed to the practice of using money as a means of dealing with the problems and anxieties of family life.

Part of the resentment of the young, Thomas Wiseman suggests in his book, *The Money Motive*, "has been of the money values to which their parents supposedly subscribe." But, says Wiseman, the grudge may be a more personal one: "It may be that, as a generation, they were weaned on bribery; that in the first heady experience of having money, many parents discovered the secret of 'shutting them up' with presents, treats, goodies, and the bought services of others. . . . . The common cry of 'but we always gave them the best,' meaning the most expensive, would seem to bear out this theory that paying out money can easily be made to serve as a substitute for human responsibility."[1]

If we tried to skirt the dangers of affluence by

[1]Thomas Wiseman, *The Money Motive* (New York: Random House, 1974).

denying our children what we could very well afford, we set ourselves up for feelings of guilt and the sense of playing a hypocritical game. There is something artificial about living in a well-appointed suburban home with two cars in the garage and a color TV in the living room while insisting that your child stay within a meager allowance. The traditional values of thrift and hard work grew out of economic necessity; the child growing up on a hardscrabble farm did not have to be coerced into doing the daily chores. But where the struggle for survival is absent, the old values become unworkable. It is farcical for parents to insist that children help clean the house or wash the dishes when there is a housekeeper coming in every day and an electric dishwasher in the kitchen. By refusing to perform unnecessary chores for the "benefit of their character," the children risk arousing their parents' anger, but they are simply declining to participate in what they perceive as a false charade.

Whichever route we took, our money values placed us and our children in the position of adversaries.

Money Values

Money intrudes itself between the generations like a spit of land between a river and its tributary. Since attitudes toward money are formed by individual and social experience, it is all but inevitable for the two generations, with their totally different economic experiences, to clash frequently and at times furiously over money matters. The values of the preaffluent and postaffluent eras stand out in bold relief when parents and children confront the subject of personal and family finance.

The parents' money values are an offshoot of their adherence to the Protestant work ethic, the basic ingredients of which are:

- Work is an end in itself, a "calling" that involves one's sense of duty. "It is an obligation," says Max Weber, "which the individual is supposed to feel and does feel towards the content of his professional activity, no matter in what it consists...."[2] And we might add, no matter how boring or unsatisfying it might be. The accumulation of money is also an end in itself, regardless of whether or not it increases the happiness and well-being of the individual.

- Thrift and sacrifice are necessary for the acquisition of money and possessions; the piling up of goods and currency certifies one's position in society.

These values have lost much of their meaning for today's young adults. Whether our children belong to the group we might characterize as "aimless" or to the "new conformists" climbing the corporate ladder, they are more likely to hold money values like these:

- Work is a means to an end, the end being enjoyment and a full, rich life. However, the work itself should be as pleasant and as free from routine and tedium as possible.

[2]Max Weber, *The Protestant Ethic and the Spirit of Capitalism* (New York: Charles Scribner, 1958).

- Money is essential for the pursuit of new sensations and experiences, which define the full, rich life.

- Money should be spent as fast, or faster, than it comes in (there's always credit), because it's worth less and less as time goes on.

In the following fairly typical conversation between a father and his twenty-four-year-old son, one can almost hear the two value systems locking horns.

FATHER: I asked you to stop by because of this note I received from Phil Harrison. He says you didn't show up for the interview.
SON: That's right.
FATHER: What happened?
SON: I went backpacking with a couple of guys and we stayed over an extra day so——
FATHER: So you missed the appointment—after I had to practically go down on my knees to Phil Harrison to arrange it for you!
SON: I'm sorry you went to all that trouble.
FATHER: Do you realize how many young people there are with MBA degrees who'd give a great deal for an opportunity like that?
SON: I don't want to spend my life in some bureaucratic trap. I've seen what that does to people.
FATHER: What do you want to do with your life?
SON: Explore. Learn everything I can learn.
FATHER: To what purpose?
SON: Why does everything have to have a purpose?
FATHER: And while you're exploring and learning, what are you going to live on? You expect me to

keep on supporting you? Do you realize how hard I've worked all my life while you've had everything handed to you?

SON: I don't need anything from you. I get along fine. A job here and there. Unemployment insurance. Food stamps.

FATHER: Where's the future in that?

SON: I don't know about the future. I'm just taking it one day at a time.

The situation is a standoff: The son is not only turning down a job—he's rejecting the life his father has been living. And the father, in return, is expressing his contempt for the son's choice of life style. When the father asks what the son is going to live *on,* he is presumably referring to money. But his question actually goes beyond that, to what his son is going to live *by.* The father remembers waiting on tables to pay his college fees; he remembers the excitement of receiving his first paycheck, the satisfaction he had in seeing the family and the bank account growing and the mortgage on the house shrinking. He recalls coming across a sentence in a book that he felt could have been written about him: "He has a sense of the merit of serviceability or efficiency and of the demerit of futility, waste, or incapacity." How is it, he wonders, that none of this has rubbed off on his son?

The son has other memories: of his father coming home late, dog-tired and preoccupied; the angry scenes between his parents, mostly over money; his mother's losing battle against alcoholism; his parents' divorce; the brittle laughter of his mother, now living in a condominium in Palm Springs; the lost, bewildered look on his father's face now and then when he catches him off guard. The son wishes his father and he could be more like—like buddies, just a couple of guys, maybe having a beer together and talking about things. There're lots of things the son would like to talk about to an older guy who'd understand. . . . Maybe then their conversation would go more like this:

FATHER: Phil Harrison tells me you didn't show up for the appointment.

SON: Yeah. Sorry you went to all that trouble about it. But the job just isn't for me.

FATHER: I guess you're right. Why should both of us get caught in the organization trap?

SON: You did okay, though. I mean—you did your best to give us a good life.

FATHER: Thanks. I appreciate that. So—do you have any plans?

SON: Only as far as next weekend. I'm going backpacking. Why don't you come along?

FATHER: Well, I was going to start on the annual report this weekend but—ah, the hell with it. Backpacking sounds great. It'll give us a chance to talk. And hey . . . you fixed all right for money?

SON: Sure. I just finished a free-lance job. That'll hold me for a while. See you Saturday, eight o'clock sharp. . . .

In this dialogue there is some give-and-take as each concedes the right of the other to hold a differing position. The father makes a concession to the son's viewpoint in his reference to "the organization trap." The son acknowledges the worth of the father's working life—which he does not want for himself—by expressing his appreciation of the father's efforts to provide a good life for his family. At the same time neither is moving away from his own position or attempting to impose it upon the other. Behind the spoken words is the mutual recognition of an existing connection between them that draws upon sources other than money.

The Money Connection

For centuries money served the purpose of keeping—at times forcing—families together. Property passed from fathers to sons and to daughters in the form of dowries. It was taken for granted that the sons would move into the fathers' occupations—as farmers, doctors, tradesmen, clergymen; the daughters' lives would also be very much like their mothers' and grandmothers'.

Among traditional families in America the individual was expected to subordinate his or her personal interest to the welfare of the family. The family, in return, was obliged to take care of the individual; there was, in fact, no alternative since the family was the only source of social security, unemployment insurance, or welfare. At one time during the depression, when the company my father worked for went bankrupt and we were in such dire financial straits that we were facing eviction from our apartment, the family rallied around and saw us through: A second cousin was located who owned an apartment building in a reasonably livable neighborhood, and he was persuaded to let us move into an unoccupied apartment and live there rent free till my father was able to find another job. An uncle in the garment

business provided for the clothing needs of my mother and me. Another uncle who owned a stationery
store took care of my school supplies. And my grandparents moved in with us, where they stayed for the
rest of their lives, drawing from their savings to cover the cost of food and other necessities. It was understood that if and when their savings were
exhausted, they would be provided for by their children.

In traditional American families and in cultures
that have not yet achieved a high level of industrial-
ization, this sort of family ethic still prevails. In fact,
economic arrangements determine the nature of
family bonds in many parts of the world. But one of
the distinctive features of American life as it has
evolved in this century is its freedom: freedom of the
individual in the choice of marriage partners, economic activity, private living quarters, and day-to-
day life, and—in a striking departure from the
past—freedom of the nuclear family from obligations to relatives and grandparents. Personal rather
than financial considerations have top priority. The
welfare of the individual comes before the welfare of
the family. Inevitably, the nuclear family has developed into a temporary arrangement, valid only as
long as it gives satisfaction to the family members.
Its structure is loose and malleable, making it sus-
ceptible to numerous reshufflings and reorganiza-
tions, in which fiscal factors play a very small part.
If Mother feels that she is being stifled within the domestic circle and must go off to "find herself" (a favorite situation in recent films and novels), who
would be crass enough to bring up the matter of finances, such as the cost of a separate dwelling, additional baby-sitting, and so on. Or if it is Father who

is impelled to seek a new path to personal growth, which at the moment has led him into the bed of his dental hygienist, could he be expected to evaluate in financial terms this glorious adventure in self-renewal? Especially since the earning power of his wife (soon to be his ex-wife) is at least equal to his?

The weakening of the economic bond in American families has been hastened by the government's assumption of financial obligations that formerly belonged to the family. If today's social climate had existed at the time of my parents' economic crisis, how very different the resolution would have been. We would have looked to unemployment insurance and welfare rather than relatives to tide us over, and my grandparents would have remained in some bleak low-cost housing development, eking out a marginal existence on their social security payments.

With the decline of economic interdependence in families, affectional ties have replaced financial ties as the primary bonds holding a family together. For this reason, as sociologist Armand Mauss notes, "Hostility and aggression on the part of family members are probably more disruptive in American families than in families in societies where economic ties are still important in holding the family unit together."[3]

Without the money connection binding their children to them, parents often feel a sense of helplessness as their sons and daughters grow up and go off to lead their own lives. Where formerly money was a language parents could rely on as a means of communication with their children, they are now left, as

[3]Armand Mauss, "Emerging Modes of Marriage" in *Social Problems as Social Movements* (Philadelphia: Lippincott, 1975).

it were, speechless when the children no longer regard money as a source of parental authority. The hostility and aggression Mauss refers to boil up in many cases when the parents attempt to use money in order to assume control over their children's adult lives. But here is a curious development typifying the crosscurrents of contemporary life: Because of the prolonged adolescence and our precarious economy, with its high rate of inflation and youth unemployment, young adults are accepting financial aid from their parents for a much longer period than in the past. However, since they reject the money values of their parents' generation, the children do not consider that their acceptance of parental support incurs any obligations on their part.

"My father is a real estate developer," said a twenty-five-year-old graduate student who is working on his Ph.D. in environmental science. "He's made a pile of money out of tearing up forests and flattening mountains. I figure what he gives me is conscience money. He owes me. It's as simple as that."

Well, maybe not so simple. Here are the parents, desperately trying to buy themselves a place in their children's lives. And there are the children, pulling out of the parents' magnetic field into their own orbit and drawing on the parents' financial resources to support their separate lives. The situation is made to order for feelings of resentment ("My son doesn't even take the trouble to thank me for the checks I send him") and suspicion ("My mother always sends me clothes as gifts. Is she being generous or is she still trying to tell me how I should dress?").

The Language of Money

Money can be either the most subtle or the most blatant carrier of messages between parents and children.

Something as seemingly innocent as the gifts we exchange with each other can carry a double meaning: They can be expressions of mutual affection or conveyors of a critical message, such as the daughter read into the clothes sent to her by her mother. Another young woman, newly married, saw her mother-in-law's gifts as a criticism of her housekeeping: "I know she thinks I'm a lousy housekeeper, but Jeff and I both work. His mother has never done anything but stay at home and clean and polish, and, anyway, there are a lot of things in the world more important to us than a shiny, clean apartment. But hardly a week goes by without the arrival of a gift package, and it's always something like a jar of English furniture wax or a package of chamois dust cloths, and last week it was a kit for cleaning windows. I guess I forgot to tell her when I married her son that I don't do windows."

On the parent side I heard few complaints about gifts received or not received from children, the usual comments being: "They're too busy" or "They really can't afford anything much" or "It's enough for us that they remember." But there was this rueful remark from a recently divorced woman in her fifties who was starting a new career in public relations and a new love affair with a younger man: "My kids don't approve of the life I'm leading. They want me to stop coloring my hair and settle down and act my age. So what did they send me for my birthday?

A book on how to be a grandmother and a sewing kit."

It's when money carries manipulative messages that the most sensitive problems arise between parents and grown children. The messages may be inspired by a sincere wish to do "what is best for the children," but the forces that are set in motion often produce scenarios like the following one:

A father is willing to underwrite a son's medical education but refuses to invest a smaller sum in a record company that the son has an opportunity to buy into. The son goes to medical school and drops out after two years. Heated father-son encounter follows, with father shouting, "Seven thousand dollars down the drain!" and the son shouting back, "You and your fucking money. From now on, you can take it and shove it."

Son joins rock band, in time becoming manager. Band hits the big time, cuts several popular discs. Son buys estate in the Hamptons and Park Avenue co-op for himself and singer-girlfriend, turns up on prime-time TV. Father's business associates congratulate him on son's success, but father hasn't seen son since the day of their stormy encounter and the only communication he's had is a check for $7,000 forwarded to him by son's business agent.

Using money manipulatively is a common ploy among divorced parents in their competition for their children's affections. A divorced mother says angrily, "My ex-husband gave our sixteen-year-old daughter a Porsche for her birthday. Now she's decided she'd rather live with him than with me. I'm not going to try to keep her against her will, but I'm thinking, maybe if I took her to Europe with me this

summer, I could change her mind. . . ." And since manipulation works both ways, maybe the daughter will
encourage her parents in this contest far into her
adult years, or as long as it continues to yield such
attractive payoffs.

Guilt Money

Was there ever a generation of parents as guilt-
ridden as ours? Not only did we bear the brunt of the
Freud/Spock philosophies and the pressures of
"making it," but we were also in the front ranks of
those who felt the full impact of mass communication with its seductive and repeated assaults upon
our impulses to consume. Television grew up along
with our children, and in the heady atmosphere of a
booming birthrate and economy, we yielded without
a struggle to the medium's message that the good
life could be bought—if not for cash, certainly on
credit. Looking ahead, we saw our children as inheritors of a standard of living that had formerly been
reserved for a small privileged group. And when, despite our acquisition of the amenities and appurte-
nances of the "good life," that happiness continued
to elude us, when the glowing promises were not fulfilled, either for us or our children, we assumed that
the failure must lie within us, that we had somehow
been unable to realize the unprecedented opportunity that had been ours. When a seventeen-year-old
boy in Orange County, California, committed suicide,
his grieving father told reporters: "He had everything going for him. He had just bought a water bed
and he had motorcycles and cars. He never wanted
for anything."

Having been convinced on all sides that it is we, the parents, who are personally responsible for whatever may have gone wrong in our children's lives, we continue to believe, many of us, that money can somehow set everything right. Parents who go on contributing indefinitely to the support of their adult children out of a sense of guilt—paying out "conscience money," as the son of the real estate developer called it—are attempting to settle a debt that can never be paid off. At least not as long as parent and child are locked in a relationship that has outlived its usefulness and is subsisting on atrophied emotions and memories.

What Do I Owe My Children?

We are uncomfortable with notions of legal and financial obligation in a relationship that we should like to think is above such crass considerations. But with the money connection extending further on into the lives of both generations, we must sooner or later confront the question of what our financial obligations are to our adult children and how these obligations can be carried out to our mutual satisfaction.

Legally, parents have a fundamental right and duty to exercise custody, care, and control in the upbringing of their children, and are required to educate them according to minimal government dictates, which vary from state to state. The general rule is that parents are not required to support children who are capable of supporting themselves or who have reached the legal age of twenty-one. But the courts may take special circumstances into account in their interpretation of the rules. In a recent New York case, a student who had reached the age of twenty-one sued her father for her college tuition and won her case. The jury found that the father had promised he would pay his daughter's tuition for the sophomore and junior years, and later reneged on his agreement when she sided with her mother during a divorce action. The manipulative message apparently came through loud and clear to the jury.

But it is the moral rather than the legal issues that are most troublesome in money questions between parents and children. Many parents take firm stands on these questions, ranging all the way from "We sustain them while they're in school and that's it" to "As long as our children need financial help from us, they're going to get it—I don't care how old they are."

Even these certainties tend to crumble in the face of specific situations. What, for example, is the appropriate parental response to the following:

· A nineteen-year-old college student who dislikes living in the dormitories asks her parents to set her up in her own apartment and provide her with a car so she can commute to campus. She understands that this is a strain on them financially, and if they can't manage it, that's okay, because the father of one of her girlfriends, a real swinger even if he is pushing sixty, has offered to provide her with the apartment and the car, and all he wants in return is to be able to stay over a couple of nights a week.

· A twenty-three-year-old sometime actor requires a substantial amount of support to keep him in the style that he feels is necessary for furthering his career. He hints that if the money isn't forthcoming any other way, "it's no sweat" because he has certain connections in the drug trade.

- A thirty-six-year-old woman, divorced three times, is about to embark on an expensive program of psychotherapy, which she is convinced will help her "get her head together," but of course, Mom and Dad will have to assist with the finances, because she's flat, stony broke. Mom and Dad are in their late sixties and are living on a shrinking retirement income.

- The eighteen-year-old daughter of devout Catholics is pregnant and desperately wants an abortion. If her parents refuse to pay for it, she's heard from a girl at school about someone who'll do it really cheap and who's as good as a regular doctor.

In each of these cases the parents, regardless of their convictions or economic philosophy, came through. The alternatives were too repugnant to contemplate. "We knew we were in a sense being blackmailed," they admitted, "but what else could we do? After all, he/she is our child."

What else could they do? What would you or I do in their place? There are no prefabricated answers or packaged formulas for dealing with questions like these. But we can try to structure the problem so that it can be moved out of an emotional morass onto a more manageable level. We can ask ourselves: What would I do if, in each case, the protagonist were a close friend rather than my child?

Suppose, then, your friend asks you for financial help and you disapprove of the use to which the money will be put. But you don't want to let your friend down, so you offer him or her a loan, not a gift, and specify terms and conditions. You also let your friend know that you are not happy about the way the money is to be used, and you offer to help him or her find a more positive direction for the future.

There are risks here, of course. You may lose your friend, or your money, or both. But there are risks in all human relationships and especially when it comes to actions that place one human being in debt to another. As Schiller's William Tell says: "That he saw me weak, he'll never forget." But there are also some important advantages in this stance. As a friend, stripped of parental fears, anxieties, and guilt, we can be more rational about our children's financial behavior. We can ask ourselves: What do we owe them, except a chance to become fully realized, self-aware, individually and socially responsible men and women? If this takes some occasional subsidizing along the way, and we can manage it without strain, then the help probably qualifies as a good investment. But if we're underwriting a course of action or a way of life that is offensive to us, our resentment and self-disgust for allowing ourselves to be exploited will pile up until an impassable barrier arises between ourselves and the recipients of our largess.

"It's the children's attitude about money that's important to me," said a university administrator who is supporting two of her four children, a twenty-three-year-old son and a twenty-five-year-old daughter. "Are they taking advantage of you? Or are they accepting it in the spirit in which it's given, as an expression of affection and respect? My children are working very hard to develop their careers—my son as a photographer, my daughter as a novelist. Supporting them seems as natural to me now as when they were little. It's all in the way you look at money. I don't associate money with self-esteem or with dependency. I don't feel that it gives me any control over my children. Only once do I remember using it for control. It was during the sixties, when our older son was at Columbia University and they were having those riots. I talked to my son on the phone and I told him, 'What you do is your own affair, but as long as I'm breaking my back to keep you there, I expect you to use your time for studying.' Aside from that one time whatever I give my kids is without strings attached. And, anyway, I could never pay them back for all they've given me."

What Do I Owe My Parents?

In the traditional family it was taken for granted that the children owed their parents everlasting devotion, respect, and physical care, if and when it was required. "Honor thy father and mother" was an unbreakable rule, and the thought that a father or mother might not deserve honoring was unthinkable. The biological act of becoming a father or mother was sufficient to command lifelong fealty and support from one's offspring.

Of course, you might dislike either or both of your parents; they might even feel the same way about you—although this idea violates the Norman Rockwell portrayal of the American family as loving and united. Whatever your personal feelings, you

were bound to each other by bonds of blood and economic necessity. As your parents had cared for you,
so you would care for them. And since pension plans
were in limited use and social security nonexistent,
parents in their post-earning years would depend either on their savings or on support from their children. However, since in premodern times compara-
tively few people lived to a ripe old age, the care of
one's parents usually occupied only a brief span in
the children's lifetime.

Today, with more people living to an old age and
the weakening of economic interdependence in the
family, the problem of parent care has taken on new
and complex dimensions. Bernice Neugarten, in a
discussion of today's middle-aged woman, makes the
point that the latter's major problem—greater than
that of her relations with children or husband, or
even of menopause or the empty nest—is parent
care. For "it is not unusual today for a forty-year-old
woman to have both a sixty-five-year-young-old
mother and an eighty-five-year-old-old grandmother
to be concerned about."[4] She may also have a twenty-two-year-old daughter who is the unmarried mother of an infant and who is attempting to complete her
college studies. It's a multilayered generation sandwich in which increasing pressure from the outer layers is exerted upon the heavily burdened middle.

How can those in the middle layer deal with the
financial demands pressing upon them from both
sides? Where should Neugarten's forty-year-old
woman invest her modest resources—on the daugh-

[4]Bernice L. Neugarten, "Midlife Women in the 1980s," *Women in Midlife—Security and Fulfillment*, Select Committee on Aging (Washing-
ton, D.C.: U.S. Government Printing Office, 1978).

ter who is eager to complete her studies so that she can eventually support herself and her child or on the widowed mother and grandmother eking out a meager existence on savings and social security stipends that are being eroded by inflation?

When, not so long ago, I found myself caught in this pincers movement, I thought of the lifeboat parable in which two middle-aged men, one an Arab, the other an American, are asked to imagine the following: "You are in a lifeboat with your mother, your wife, and your child, and the boat capsizes. You can save yourself and only one of the remaining three. Whom will you save?"

The American, after a certain amount of anguished soul searching, replies that he would save the child. The Arab, with no hesitation, says that he would save the mother, reasoning, "You can have more than one wife in a lifetime, you can have more than one child, but you have only one mother. You must save your mother."

Here is a stark and dramatic contrast in cultural values between the product of a society that looks to the future and one that looks to the past. But the same contrast can be found between two different age groups within the same society—our own. When the parable was presented to a class of one hundred freshmen in a problem-solving course, sixty responded in favor of the child and forty the wife. When the professor asked whether anyone would save the mother, there was a roar of laughter.[5]

For those brought up with the traditional values it hurts too much when we laugh. For us, past, pres-

[5]Moshe F. Rubinstein, *Patterns of Problem Solving* (New Jersey: Prentice-Hall, 1975).

ent, and future flow together in a continuum, so that
when our lifeboat capsizes, we flail about frantically,
trying to save parent, spouse, and child. And our aging parents, however much they may protest that
they don't want to be a burden to us, have been nourished and have nourished us on the principle that, as
the parent cared for the child, so the child will one
day care for the parent. It is a principle that transcends legal or even personal considerations.

"My father and I never got along," said a woman in her fifties, an industrial psychologist who has
children and grandchildren and a ninety-year-old father. "He's always been totally selfish, spent lavish-
ly on himself and never gave a damn about anyone
unless they were useful to him. Even when I was little, I saw him as a phony and a manipulator, and I
don't remember his ever saying a kind or loving
word to me." Nevertheless, he feels, and she agrees,
that she is responsible for him, and she has added another consulting assignment to her already overpres-
sured life so that she can provide him with something approximating his accustomed standard of
living.

To extricate ourselves from the generational
sandwich requires a cooperative approach at all levels to the economics of our respective situations.
Freeing ourselves from our parental and filial ties
can also free us to assess our financial situation realistically. Here, we can say, are the available resources. What is the most rational way to allocate
them? When we deal with each other as sensible
adults engaged in a mutual-assistance endeavor, the
question of what we owe our parents or our children
can be removed from the usual emotion-laden atmosphere and negotiated in a reasonable and pragmatic

manner. This approach may not resolve all our financial problems in one fell swoop, but it will increase
our chances of working them out amicably and of
distributing the burdens more equitably.

Willing the Future

"I declare this to be my last will and testa-
ment . . ." These words, or similar legal phraseology,
begin the document with which parents can continue
to influence their children's financial future. Drawing up a will is the ultimate parental act of self-con-
frontation. When it becomes necessary to establish,
in cold legal terms, the means by which your life's
accumulation will be distributed after you are dead,
all the delusions and pretenses are stripped away.
You may have been assuring yourself that Eric is beginning to settle down and learning the value of a
dollar; that Janey's current live-in boyfriend, whom,
like all the others, she is subsidizing, at least bears
some resemblance to a member of the human species; that Billy may be a pothead and somewhat irresponsible, but after all he did manage to hold on to
a job for almost two months. But when you come to
the point of bequeathing what you have worked so
hard for all your life, it is difficult to maintain any
degree of self-deception about those who will be your
heirs. A successful businessman said, "I don't want
my sons, whom I love very much, to inherit my estate. I don't trust them with it. For their own good
I'm setting up my will so that they receive a modest
income instead of getting all of it at once."
The practice of establishing trusts for one's children is an admission that we don't trust them to use

and invest money wisely. And, in fact, there is some evidence that today's generation of young adults show a "proclivity to consume inheritances" instead of investing them—a tendency entirely in keeping with the new values.

Nevertheless, the urge to keep money in the family by handing it on to the children is a powerful one, and practical speculations about what the children might do with their inheritance are not likely to act as a deterrent. Parents who have known poverty and have struggled to gain a measure of wealth are often bent on liberating their children from a similar struggle for survival. Money, these parents argue, will give their children freedom of choice. "If I had had that freedom," said a hard-working manufacturer, "I could have been a concert pianist, or a poet, or a pure mathematician instead of a businessman."

There are also some disadvantages. The children never throw off the feeling that they are living off their parents, which can be damaging to their development. They may never be sure about their friends or their lovers: "Is it me or my money that's the attraction?" And they may lack that spur to achieve that money so often provides; as a study of the economics of inheritance concludes: "Inheritance tends both to increase the incentive to earn of people allowed to transfer wealth while decreasing the incentive to earn of those seeking the wealth."[6]

The stipulations of a will can also have long-term effects on family relationships. When one child receives more than another, or the spouse receives the entire estate while the children receive nothing,

[6]"The Economics of Inheritance and Its Restrictions: A Practical Proposal," *UCLA Law Review*, 22 (1974–75).

the resulting resentments may poison the relationships among the children or between the children and the remaining parent for the rest of their lives.

There are also special problems that arise when a child inherits the parent's business. If the son or daughter taking over the business proves to be incompetent, as is frequently the case, it is much more difficult to oust the incapable inheritor of a business than an incompetent hired employee.

But when all is said and done, the attempt to control our children's lives from the grave is an exercise in futility, even more so than the effort to control them while we are alive after they have achieved adulthood. As ex-parents, our will should reflect what we honestly believe is in the best interests of those to whom we are connected, not by money, and not by obligation, but by the ties of close and caring friendship.

PART III

Finished and Unfinished Business

I left behind me a young man who
did not have time to be my father
and who could now be my son. . . .

—Jean-Paul Sartre, *The Words*

8
Under One Roof

The experiences of parents and adult children who live together leave no doubt that the sharing of a domicile is a critical factor in the transformation of the parent-child connection into the bond of friendship. Moving on to the next stage in the cycle of relationships is accomplished with fewer strains and tensions when there is some physical as well as psychological distance between parent and child.

On this score family counselors and psychologists are virtually unanimous, and most of us who are parents of adult children would readily agree. It doesn't require any special expertise to recognize that, in today's world, two generations under one roof makes for a highly combustible mixture, one in which the volatile elements aren't easily separated. We are told that nineteen is the average age for leaving home in America, and we take it as a given that this rite of passage is essential for achieving independence and responsibility. But acceptance of what we regard as the facts doesn't automatically translate them into a workable reality.

When our children reach leaving-home age, we put on a brave face and wave them cheerfully on their way. But their empty rooms evoke an emptiness within us, and we wait impatiently for their letters, phone calls, visits home. "My children's rooms are exactly as they were when they were living at home," I was told by a woman whose children are twenty-six, twenty-eight, and thirty-two. Does she realize, I wondered, what those intact rooms are saying about her longings and fantasies?

The Adult Child in Residence

Clinging to the Nest

My explorations turned up two basic variations on the nesting theme. In one we have adult children who show no inclination to leave home, even long past the customary age, and who resist all parental efforts to push them out. These "nesters" usually give as their reasons the need to establish clearer career goals or to gain a firmer financial foothold. A twenty-four-year-old musician says he would rather continue living at home, pursuing temporarily a financially unrewarding career as a music writer and rock-band member, than work at a nine-to-five job just to pay the rent. A twenty-three-year-old law student prefers the domestic order and amenities of her parents' suburban home to a "grubby apartment that I'd have to take care of myself." A thirty-year-old who has been working on his Ph.D. for the past six years lives with his divorced mother, who pays all the expenses so that her son can devote himself full-time to his studies.

Well, after all, what could be more sensible? Why should our children, whatever their age, struggle and deny themselves to keep a roof over their heads when there's a perfectly good roof available for them in the home we've always shared? But, when you probe behind the rationalizations, you frequently find that money is only part of the story, and that, particularly in middle- to high-income families, it often serves as a camouflage for other needs.

The mother of that twenty-three-year-old law student says that she and her husband have repeatedly offered to set their daughter up in an apartment for which they are willing to pay the rent, utilities, and even the cost of a cleaning service. She adds, "And she can have her meals here whenever she wants to," but the daughter consistently refuses their offers. Why? "Because," says her mother, "she is afraid to strike out on her own. She feels safer living with us, among familiar surroundings—but it makes it very difficult to establish an adult relationship with her. No matter how much freedom we give her, there are always the ties and memories of the past. I feel we won't be able to enjoy each other until she moves out. There's no way we can develop a real friendship under these conditions. She has a very different tone with us than with her friends. With us, she's still the little girl." The mother concludes, after a moment's reflection, "I guess we overprotected her."

There are, on the other hand, parents who claim to be entirely satisfied with such an arrangement. The father of the twenty-four-year-old musician is obviously pleased to have his son staying on at home:

"Having him at home keeps us young. His friends come over, and they have parties and play music and the house is always lively." And the mother of the thirty-year-old Ph.D. candidate says, somewhat defensively, "In this society you're made to feel there's something wrong if your children go on living with you after they're grown up. My son and I give each other plenty of space. We enjoy being together. It makes good sense financially. I don't see anything wrong with it."

Going Home Again

The other side of the coin is the adult child who leaves home and then returns, presumably disproving the you-can't-go-home-again dogma. Money—the inflationary rise in rent and other necessities—is also offered as the main reason by those who have left the fold and returned. But, again, there is usually more to it than simple economics. For many of these "returnees," leaving home was a mixed bag, containing equal parts of euphoria and despair. There was the eager clutch at autonomy—going away to school, finding a job, furnishing an apartment of one's own—followed by the sobering confrontation with loneliness, the grinding routine of college or a job, and the relentless pressure of meeting financial obligations. A point is reached at which the comforts and security of the parental home begin to appear so alluring that the adult child gives up on the effort at self-sufficiency and moves back.

Depending upon how it is handled, this return home can represent a serious setback to the separation-individuation process through which we evolve into ex-parents and ex-children. But as psychoanalyst Margaret Mahler and her co-workers point out, "Smooth and consistently progressive personality development is rendered exceedingly difficult by the exquisite complexity of the human being's task to adapt as a separate individual to the ever-increasing dangers of living in a contaminated and essentially hostile world."[1]

The grown child who remains at home or who returns after leaving may be an adult according to chronological age, but without having achieved the full development of adulthood. Growing up, as we've noted, varies widely depending on the individual's own chemistry, the values of the society, and the temper of the times. Today, in our complex and highly developed society, it takes more time than formerly for the young to mature and prepare themselves sufficiently to confront a "contaminated and essentially hostile world." This means that parents must walk a fine line between forcing their children out of the nest too soon and keeping them there past the time when they are ready for independence. This exercise in timing requires that we be on the alert for signals from our children and that we respond to these signals from the stance of a loving friend. Some signs to watch for include the live-in child becoming moody and restless; increasing frequency of arguments and disagreements about details of daily living; rising level of frustration on both sides; a child's suggestion that it might be a good idea to find a job, finish law school at night, and share an apartment with a couple of friends. Alert parents who are moving toward ex-parenthood will heed such signs

[1]Mahler, Pine, and Bergman, *The Psychological Birth of the Human Infant* (New York: Basic Books, 1975).

and cooperate with their adult children's plans for breaking away, giving them whatever emotional and temporary financial support they may need.

Some parents who have been through the experience maintain that it is easier to develop an amicable and egalitarian connection with adult children who leave home and return than with those who have not yet made the break. Even a brief taste of independence, it seems, can speed up and smooth for both generations the process of disconnecting themselves from obsolete roles and the behaviors that go with them. But there are others, among both parents and children, who are not so sure. The return home can stir up past conflicts and resentments. Hostilities that were cooling off begin heating up again. Former habits, attitudes, and modes of communication that may have been phasing out reassert themselves.

"I left home when I was eighteen," says a twenty-six-year-old who recently returned to her parents' home after her divorce, "and I sort of looked forward to moving back with mom and dad. Emotionally, I was a mess after my husband and I split up, and I thought it would be great living with the two people in the world who really know me and care about me. I also thought we'd reached the point where we could deal with each other as responsible adults—I mean, I'd lived on my own for five years before I was married and I've supported myself, not to mention going through a marriage and divorce. . . . But you'd think I was still a little girl who'd never been away. It's the same old routine all over again: 'Did you make your bed?' 'What time will you be getting home?' And the hell of it is, if I left them now, it would be like having another divorce. There's so much feeling mixed up in it—I mean, the way we care for each other and yet the way we grate on each other's nerves."

In the struggle to live harmoniously with an adult child who has returned to the nest, we attempt to push away the intrusive question: Whose home is it? When I visited my daughter in San Francisco, she told me that she wanted to leave college in order to have time to sort things out. I said, yes, that's a good idea, and asked, hesitantly, if she planned to stay on in San Francisco. She said, "I want to go home." I put my arms around her and held her tight, thinking how fragile she seemed, how vulnerable, while my mind dwelled already on the nourishing meals I would serve her, the new outfit I would buy for her at Magnin's.

"That's it," I said. "You're going home." For the moment neither of us remembered that what was home for me was no longer home for her.

Whose Home Is It?

Home, for adults, is a place that they have created for themselves and that reflects their tastes, interests, and life style. Adult children living with their parents may make attempts to adapt their parents' home to themselves, but this effort is rarely successful. At best the child is given a free hand with his or her room, but the rest of the home bears the distinctive mark of those who created and maintained it over the years. This may suggest why, according to a recent paper presented to the American Psychological Association, the loneliest people are not singles living alone, as is commonly assumed, but adults living with their parents.

Adult children receive a false picture of the
world when they are made to believe that the parents' home is theirs for the asking without their having to make any contribution to it. In the real world
of adult life, homes are not available on this basis;
sooner or later the adult child will have to confront
this reality, and the longer the reality is postponed,
the more painful the confrontation will be. A woman
I have known for many years, a widow who is planning to remarry, lives with her two daughters, who
are both in their twenties, one of whom is studying
acting, the other singing. Their mother would like to
sell the house and use the proceeds toward a new
house in which she and her new husband can start
afresh. "There are too many ghosts in this place,"
she says of the house to which she came as a young
bride and in which she raised her family and nursed
her husband during his last illness.

The daughters want to go on living in the house
where they were born and grew up, and are bitter
about their mother's decision. "It's our house as
much as yours," they say. "You've always told us
that." My friend is torn apart by her dilemma. The
house is legally hers, and yet: "I can't turn them out
into the street, can I? My own children ..."—her
voice trembles and she seems on the verge of tears—
"but Robert and I agreed that we would pool our
funds and buy our dream house.... I don't know
what to do."

Meanwhile the marriage is being delayed until
some solution to the problem suggests itself. Maybe
the girls will marry, although they seem to be in no
hurry to do so. Or maybe they will become self-sup-
porting and move into a place of their own, although
this also does not seem to be an imminent possibility.

Eventually, their mother and stepfather will probably finance an apartment for them, the house will be sold, and life will go on. But will mother and daughters continue to be haunted by their own ghosts—of guilt and betrayal—which they may never be able to exorcise completely? Wouldn't it have been kinder to the daughters and more agreeable all around if their mother had let them know gently but firmly that the house was her home, not theirs, and that one day they would find their satisfactions in creating homes of their own?

The Rules of the House

The traditional rules that made it possible for two or even three generations to live together have vanished into the past. In the household in which I grew up, it was accepted without question that my grandfather was the reigning authority. My mother and grandmother deferred to him in every respect, catered to his wants, trembled at his displeasure. He was the final court of appeal, and all conflicts and disputes were referred to him. It was he who determined that his youngest daughter, my Aunt Ada, should divorce her husband, who had confessed to committing adultery; and though my Uncle Mike pleaded with his wife to give him another chance, my grandfather was adamant. The divorce went through, Ada moved in with us, and for the rest of her life she devoted herself to the duties of a daughter and the satisfactions of a doting aunt.

Recalling that world that is gone forever, I realize that my grandfather's absolute rule left no room for other male contenders. My gentle, self-indulgent father was no match for this old-world patriarch, for whom he had a deep affection and respect. Years later, when my grandfather was dead, I understood, as I never had when I was a child, why it was necessary for my father to put such vast stretches of time and distance between himself and the family he cherished and of which he was inordinately proud.

Whatever doubts we may have had about each other, we were clear about the rules—and each of us knew our place in the scheme of things. The generations were stacked up in an orderly hierarchy, with the elders at the top, their children, our parents, in the middle, and the young ones at the bottom. When my grandfather died, my mother took over his role, my frail little grandmother being unqualified by nature and background to act as tribal leader. And life went on pretty much as before, with a matriarchal in place of a patriarchal ruler.

It was a benevolent despotism, intended for the good of the governed, and the house rules had about them an aura of sacrosanct inviolability, rather like the Sermon on the Mount. The home was my mother's turf, a place where her sovereignty went unchallenged even after I began contributing a substantial portion of my salary to the household expenses. My mother set the rules, which governed most aspects of our lives, and we either followed them or found ways to get around them without her knowledge.

I defied my mother openly only once, when upon discovering, a few days before my wedding day, that the divorce of my husband-to-be lacked religious sanction, she delivered a ukase: "The wedding is off." I went into my room and started packing. My mother had a hurried consultation with my Aunt Ada and appeared at the doorway to my room as I was struggling to close the bulging suitcase. "It's all right," she said. "We'll go on with it. It's not what I would want for you, but we'll go ahead. I only hope God will understand—and forgive."

It was her home all right, but it was there to offer us—all three generations—shelter, nourishment, and a rockbound sense of security that I have never experienced since. We left when it was time to marry or, in the case of the boys, to enter the service. It was understood, however, that home would always be there, whenever we wanted or needed to return; the same rules would, of course, continue to apply as would the status of the relationships. Age could not wither nor custom stale this generational connection. It was an unchanging bond in a stable universe, a world that we thought would never change.

A Live-Together Contract

With authority no longer residing in the elders, and home no longer a settled place governed by commonly accepted principles, who makes the rules today when parents and adult children share a home? The adult child who stays in the nest or returns to it usually expects Mamma to go on cooking the meals, doing the laundry, tidying up, and so on, just as she did in the past. Our sons and daughters may have been on their own for years, attending to all their needs with admirable efficiency. The moment they return to our home, they and we slip back into our former rituals and routines. A psychologist and family counselor, Isobel Dalali, offers a familiar scenario from her counseling experience, that of the twenty-seven-year-old son returning to his parent's home after several years on his own, going to the kitchen, opening the refrigerator door, and yelling in the direction of the living room, where his mother is entertaining a friend, "Ma—there's nothing to eat in this house." Whereupon Ma replies guiltily, "I'm sorry, darling, I didn't have time to do any shopping today. I'll do it first thing tomorrow."

But supposing Ma, like so many women her age, is studying full-time at college or, like 49 percent of today's American women, is working at a job or managing a business. In the real world of today, what are the rules that determine areas of domestic responsibility, and who sets out the guidelines? Without precedents to follow, there is a strong temptation to lapse back into earlier modes of behavior and communication, whether or not they are applicable to the present facts of our lives. But the attempt to live by rules that are out of touch with reality can bring on a severe case of emotional dissonance and destroy any possibility for intergenerational harmony.

Searching for a new set of hard-and-fast rules is very likely to be a fruitless quest. Our rapidly changing time is like a perpetual-motion machine, continually whirring and stirring up everything within reach before it has a chance to settle. We may never again be able to depend upon a firm set of moral precepts to provide an unshakable basis for human interaction. A state of transition is beginning to seem like the natural order of things.

The absence of rigid rules can be an advantage for parents and adult children who are, for good and sufficient reasons, making a home together. Without ironclad customs or traditions to fall back on, the burden is on us, as individuals, to develop our own rules and regulations. This involves us in a continual process of negotiation and arbitration, a flexible give-and-take that keeps all decisions open to reassessment and renegotiation according to the changing requirements of the situation. What this amounts to is a variable "contract," not a written document but simply an understanding between the parties regarding the privileges and responsibilities on either side.

Dr. Dalali, who has helped parents and grown children develop such contracts for living together, suggests that the terms should include, at a minimum, a trade-off of services and an exchange of hard capital on either side. Otherwise, she says, living at home is "suckling at the breast," and the weaning process can be a delicate and difficult business. Parents and adult children who share a home should think of each other as "roommates." Addressing herself to parents, Dr. Dalali asks, "Would you or your sons or daughters expect their roommates to pick up after them, do their laundry, cook their meals, and, on top of all that, foot the bill for all expenses?"

But: "A contract with my children?" "How can I take money from my own kids?" The voice of the Parent is heard in these typical responses to the contract idea. And yet we live in a society in which exploitation of any one group by any other is frowned upon, and in which money is the mark of value given and received. There are feminists who maintain that wives are unpaid workers in their husbands' house and that women should bargain for some kind of business contract protecting their interests, particularly in the case of divorce. As more and more women leave the home to enter the business and professional world, the idea of an understanding between men and women living together with or without benefit of clergy is gaining wider acceptance as a rational approach to present-day realities.

Among parents and children, however, the emotional usually outweighs the rational. As a result, living together keeps the two generations in a state of constant uncertainty and confusion, in which the most trivial events of daily living can set off resounding repercussions of resentment. In the list of grievances that pit parents and adult children against each other, the most common appear to be:

Parents	*Adult Children*
Hogging telephone.	Hogging telephone.
Leaving bathroom in mess.	Overemphasis on cleanliness and order.
Playing rock music at deafening level.	Inability to appreciate any music since Brahms.
Smoking pot.	Okaying booze, but vetoing pot.
Eating at odd hours; leaving dishes in sink.	Rigid mealtimes and washing up.
Inviting friends to dinner without notice.	Too much planning, no room for spontaneity.
Coming home at all hours.	Monitoring comings and goings.
Borrowing clothes and other possessions without asking.	Exaggerated concern for possessions; too materialistic.
Criticizing ideas, values, life style.	Criticizing ideas, values, life style.

Is there any hope of reconciling differences like these? Certainly not by hurling accusations back and forth—or by taking the other tack and suffering in stony, martyred silence. The grievances listed above are precisely the kinds of issues that call for negotiation and compromise. Here, for example, are terms and conditions that parents might propose:

- Let's install a separate telephone—and share the cost.

- We clean up after ourselves and share other cleaning chores, but without becoming fanatical about it.

- Music is to be played at a normal-decibel level, and not when it interferes with anyone's sleep or concentration.

- If you want to smoke pot outside of the house, that's your business.

- We can live with snacking at odd hours, if that's what you like to do, but clearing up after yourself is a rule of the house.

- Inviting friends home for dinner without notice is okay on the following conditions: You do the necessary marketing and help prepare the meal.

- As an adult you have a right to come and go as you please; we'll refrain from harassing you about this and trust you to conduct yourself responsibly.

- When you want to borrow any of our stuff, ask yourself how you would go about this if we

were your friends or roommates instead of
your parents.

· Let's respect each other's differences and try
to understand our varying attitudes and values.

The ability to strike a bargain that satisfies both
sides will depend upon how far parent and adult child
have progressed toward their new relationship as
friends and equals. The rate of progress, to express
it in mathematical terms, appears to be proportionate
to the amount of space or privacy the parties to the
arrangement grant each other.

The Right to Privacy

The overriding need—and the one most difficult
to achieve for generations living together—is that of
privacy. After so many years of our lives being tightly interlaced, we can easily lose the knack of giving
each other the space, time, and opportunity for a separate and private existence. I have met parents who
have gone to considerable trouble and expense to
satisfy this need by converting a garage into a separate apartment or building a separate entrance to
the room occupied by their son or daughter. Non-
homeowning parents have been known to rent larger
apartments to accommodate their adult children or,
if this was not possible, to provide locks and keys for
their rooms.

But psychological privacy is at least as important as physical privacy, and requires more effort,
particularly on the parents' side. When the children
were small, their lives were transparent; there were
no dark or hidden places for us—the recipients of
their thoughts and confidences—to wonder about.

The symbiosis between child and mother produced a sense of being part of each other's lives, of sharing a developing perception of the world.

Though the drive toward separation and individuation is in force in infancy (the awareness of separateness as an individual develops by the fifteenth month), the parent, especially the mother, who has nurtured the child, is rarely prepared for her child's emergence as a complex being with a private existence of his or her own. The longing to return to that earlier time when all was clear and open between parent and child is expressed as an incessant probing and prying—"poking about in my psyche," as one twenty-eight-year-old daughter in residence describes it.

When there is geographical distance between parent and child, the problem of privacy usually takes care of itself. But, when sharing a home, the physical proximity places especial importance on psychological distance, which must be created by the individuals involved. A primary requisite is the development of parental trust and confidence in the adult son or daughter, an attitude that often bolsters the child's self-confidence and self-esteem. From this attitudinal vantage point, it should be easier to resist the temptation to press for such information as:

- Who was that you were just talking to on the phone?
- When did you get in last night?
- Why don't you ever see Don (or Donna) anymore?
- How much money did you spend on those jeans?

- When did you last comb your hair?

- Why do you read those filthy books?

Living with adult children is probably the greatest challenge for ex-parents and ex-children as well as a severe testing of their ability to move away from the earlier connection. But if both parties to the "contract" live up to its terms and negotiate fairly with each other, they should be able to meet the challenges and pass the test with flying colors.

My daughter's return home lasted almost a year, a time during which we struggled toward some neutral ground where we could meet without wounding each other. There were moments when we almost succeeded, when we came close to connecting as woman to woman. But at the critical instant we—more often, I—would beat a hasty retreat, back to the false security of the Parent and Child connection.

The invitation to visit England came from a British publisher she met in Hollywood. There was the possibility of an editorial job with his firm in London and the lure of travel and adventure. England? So far away. She was so young, so inexperienced, so impulsive and impressionable. But of course she must go. There was no denying the radiance that suffused her being.

At the airport I watched her walk toward the plane, a slim, pretty girl who carried so much of me within her, just as I carried so much of her within me. As she reached the steps of the plane she turned and waved. I waved back. This time I knew she was leaving my home forever and was on the way toward creating a home and a life of her own.

9
Parents Once Removed

When I think of my grandparents, I see two very old people, my grandfather tall, erect, carrying himself with all the poise and dignity conferred by the years and by his position as head of the family; my grandmother small and wizened, her days occupied with food gathering and preparation and the never-ending demands of religious observance. All the time that I was growing up I thought of them as ancient and, at the same time, ageless; I could not imagine that they had ever been young, eager, passionate. They seemed to me frozen in time as elderly people, entitled as if by hereditary right to reverence and affection.

I have been discovering that the memory I have of my mother's parents is widely shared, especially among those whose grandparents were immigrants. Barbara Myerhoff, in her book, *Number Our Days*, writes of the Ukrainian grandmother who raised her: "As a child, I remember thinking that she had always been old. She liked being old, liked her 'drapes' as she called her wrinkles, liked being stout and thought her long hair made her look dignified. She was a 'bobbe,' a grandmother, and a 'balebosteh,' a matron or householder. . . .Wisdom, humor and certain slowly acquired skills were the natural rewards of aging for her. . . .Her common sense, her great comfortable strength, her good health and her inner poise were sources of pride."[1]

Our grandparents were models for us of old age as a state of being with its own satisfactions and rewards. They presided at family occasions—birthdays, anniversaries, and the like—and at holiday festivities the clan came around to honor them, to praise my grandmother's cooking, and listen respectfully to my grandfather's opinions on politics, economics, and the general state of the world. They were integral to our lives, it was as if they were a projection of our budding identities—this was how it would be when we were old.

The "New Grandparent"

The conditions that produced that archetypal grandparent are gone forever, and, except for a throwback here and there, so are the grandparents who came out of that mold. When I was thinking of my grandparents as venerable, they were somewhere in their midfifties. For their time this was old age. They had married in their teens, and by their early twenties they were parents of five children, had made the long and difficult voyage from Russia

[1]Barbara Myerhoff, *Number Our Days* (New York: E.P. Dutton, 1979)

to the United States, and were busy establishing themselves in the new country. From a contemporary view, their life cycle has a foreshortened youth and an early, extended old age. They were grandparents at about the age when many adults today are still trying to decide whether or not to marry and have a family.

Psychological and physiological changes in the aging process have produced new species of grandparents: youthful, vigorous, resourceful, many of them living alone due to divorce or the death of their spouse. You see them everywhere: on tennis courts and jogging trails, in college classrooms, discos, singles bars, bistros, airports. And now and then you can even catch a glimpse of them accompanied by small children, for most of them are fond of their grandchildren and pleased to see them, when a visit fits into their schedule.

Who is this "new grandparent," and how does grandparenting in the 1980s affect the connection between parents and adult children? To begin with, the term "grandparent" can be misleading unless we divide it into grand*mothers* and grand*fathers*, for, despite unisex trends of today, there are important differences between the two.

Grandmothers have a stronger sense of obligation to their grandchildren; they feel as though they ought to help out with baby-sitting and other child-raising activities. They are also more sensitive than their male counterparts to the kind of image they present to their grandchildren. Single grandmothers, I have found, prefer not to bring their lovers to family occasions; single grandfathers generally feel no such constraint.

As these few clues suggest, today's grandmother is more vulnerable to role conflicts than the male of the species. She is a woman living in two worlds: one, to paraphrase Matthew Arnold, which is dying, the other struggling to be born. She is trying to break out of old stereotypes while clinging to the security blanket of family traditions. A grandmother I know who, at forty-eight, has established a highly successful marketing research business, is currently involved in two affairs: one with a man of her own age, the other with a man several years younger. Her two main concerns are keeping her two lovers from learning about each other, and keeping her married children from learning about either one. "They wouldn't be able to deal with it," she says. "They have other ideas about how a grandmother should behave. I'm afraid if they found out, they'd keep me away from the children. They'd consider me a bad influence."

The desexualization of the parent is pushed to its furthest limits when the parent achieves the state of grandparenthood, particularly on the female side. The mass media have decreed that women reach sexual obsolescence somewhere around forty. (It used to be thirty, but, thanks to health foods, jogging, and models like Jeanne Moreau and Lauren Bacall, the age limit has been raised.) The double standard of aging makes men in their fifties and sixties appear virile while women of the same age are considered sexual rejects. This puts the grandmother whose sexual appetites are undiminished in a double bind: The men who would normally be her sex partners are involved with younger women; the men who are old enough to be available for her are usually at the low ebb of their sexual powers. In addition, she must deal with the guilt and embarrassment she feels at what she realizes is generally looked upon as inappropriate behavior for a grandmother.

As "new grandparents," male or female, we differ from the traditional rocking-on-the-porch model in another important respect: We are no longer the pillars of the family structure. That cozy picture of parents and children arriving at their grandparents' house for the holidays is gradually receding from present-day reality. Our adult children may be dispersed all over the globe so that we rarely get together for ceremonial occasions or other events. Many of us settle for an exchange of cards and gifts at birthdays and Christmas.

But even more than the factor of geographical distance, our adulation of youth and our emphasis on individual fulfillment do not promote lasting intergenerational ties. There are some grandparents who feel closer to their grandchildren than to their children, but I have come across many more who admit that they feel irrelevant to their grandchildren's lives and, increasingly, to the lives of their children, as their married sons and daughters become absorbed with parenthood.

Here is a brief excerpt from a conversation between psychoanalyst Anne Steinmann and her eleven-year-old granddaughter, Abby:

ANNE: Do your friends discuss their grandparents?

ABBY: No. They don't say too much; they say their grandparents gave them this or something like that, but they don't say much.

ANNE: They never talk about how their grandparents feel about certain things or that their grandparents have certain ideas?

ABBY: Not really.

ANNE: Suppose you moved to Alaska, would you feel that your life would go on, that there would be no blank?

ABBY: Yes.

One of the grandparents I interviewed said, "Grandparents today are disposable." Her comment aroused in me a dormant memory of a Christmas day some years ago when an engagement for the following morning made it necessary for me to leave a family gathering in our mountain cottage and make my way by bus to Los Angeles. It was a dismal day, cold and rainy, and I remember thinking as I looked about me at the few people on the bus that these were surely the hopelessly displaced, alone and in transit, when they should have been gathered around a fireplace with their families. Across the aisle dozed a man who appeared to be in his early sixties. His skin was the color and texture of Gorgonzola cheese, and the rhythmic rasping coming from his chest suggested, possibly, emphysema. Is he a father? I wondered. A grandfather? Where is he going? Where has he come from?

The woman sitting beside me broke into my thoughts. "I've been on a job," she said, in the abrupt and confidential manner that strangers on public conveyances adopt when they initiate a conversation. "I've been taking care of an elderly woman. Now I'm on my way home to Los Angeles. I do a lot of odd jobs—baby-sitting, waitressing, whatever I can find to get along."

I nodded, at a loss for an appropriate response. I guessed that she was in her late fifties; she looked like one of those sturdy, well-put-together no-nonsense women who grow up on farms in the Middle West. "I used to work for the University of Chicago," she went on. "I have a son who's a professor at Syracuse and another one a lawyer in Boston. I have six sons and fourteen grandchildren." The statement was made matter-of-factly.

This time I responded with a question that came tumbling out, before I could judge its appropriateness. "May I ask why, with a family like that, you are alone on Christmas day?"

"Well—" She watched the rain slithering down the window—"My car was stolen last week and my winter coat was in it. I didn't want to fly into the cold weather without a warm coat and I just couldn't find anything I really liked.... And besides," she said after a slight pause, "they're scattered all over the country. I could only visit one of them, and if I did that, the others would be jealous, you see."

The disposable, or surplus, grandparent is beginning to appear even in Hispanic, black, and other minority groups, in which the traditional role for the elders has been a cornerstone of the culture. It seems clearer every day that the role of grandparent, as we have known it, is another victim of social change in our time. With the disappearance of the traditional grandparent, and all the trappings of custom and ritual that shored up that family connection, there are many who, after the birth of their first grandchild, feel oddly disoriented, as if they were drifting with neither compass nor anchor. For the "new grandparents," ambiguity and social insecurity are part of the price they must pay for the dismantling of tradition and the shattering of former stereotypes.

The Grandparents' Identity Crisis

You hold in your arms a tiny addition to the human stream, and while marveling at the miracle of it, you wonder: What, really, are we to each other? This strangely familiar little creature carries within it some ineffable part of you, is DNA-coded with some of your genes. You have a sense of *déjà vu,* of having been here before—there are echoes from another time, another existence. Long-buried sensations resurrect themselves as you relive your first experience of shock and wonder at becoming a parent.

But this time you are not a parent. You are something less, something more, something different—a parent once removed. Between you and this miniature human being stand the real parents, your son or daughter and his or her mate. They link you to your grandchild; they also separate you. Where do you really belong in this new generational construct?

"When my first grandchild was born, I was thrown into an identity crisis," is what I heard from several of the grandparents I interviewed. "I couldn't imagine what was expected of me." And even after several grandchildren have arrived on the scene and are growing out of childhood: "I'm still not sure. . . . Do my children want me to spend more or less time with my grandchildren? Do they think I am too interfering—or not sufficiently interested? Are they jealous when their children are affectionate toward me—or pleased?"

Becoming a grandparent affects not only our relationship with the adult children who placed us in that role but also our sense of who we are. A recurring refrain, especially from grandparents in their forties or fifties is: "I don't feel like a grandparent.

I'm too young. I'm not ready for it." And, in fact, as it often turns out, they are *not* ready for it. Since they have not yet worked their way out of parenthood, being thrust into grandparenthood is a psychological shock. They may even secretly resent their children for doing this to them now, before they are "ready."

These are the grandparents I would classify as Rejecters. They are less concerned with their new role in the family than with their new concept of themselves. In a society that, despite progressive ideas about aging, still equates "grandparent" with "old," they see themselves being stamped as "senior citizens," in the patronizing euphemism of bureaucracy, as human discards with nothing to look forward to except deterioration and decline.

Rejecters often gravitate toward another group of "new grandparents," the Swingers, and along the way become prime prospects for plastic surgery, hair transplanting, health farms, Balkan rejuvenating clinics—whatever formulas and nostrums promise to help them postpone the inevitability of growing old. Once they have become full-fledged Swingers, they can be heard casually discussing their tennis scores, jogging mileage, and indulgence in various forms of kinky sex; what you will not hear them discussing is their grandchildren.

Whichever group these new grandparents fall into, their struggle for self-discovery and self-definition grows out of their need to develop a satisfying connection with their children, who now have children of their own.

The Changing Connection

When my daughter was born, the relationship between my mother and me remained exactly as it had always been. Having never moved out of our parent-child connection, we were not likely to do so now. There was nothing at the time that prodded us toward any change in our dealings with each other. My mother took up her new role with zest and total fidelity to the traditional model of grandmother, which nothing in her experience or in the world around her gave her any reason to question. She doted and fussed, advised, hovered, scolded, showed off photos, swapped stories with other grandmothers, and haunted Bloomingdale's infant-wear department, from which a stream of gifts flowed steadily toward my baby daughter.

As for me, I played my part as if I'd been rehearsing for it all my life. I was now the daughter in good standing who, whatever my past sins or omissions, had achieved what was expected of me and, in doing so, had bestowed upon my mother the crowning fulfillment of her life. And there was an unexpected bonus: We now had a new and apparently inexhaustible topic of conversation. No more uncomfortable silences while we rummaged in our mental scrap bags for some tattered remnant of family gossip to work over once again. Never more would I have to listen to repetitions of the tedious doings of aunts, uncles, and cousins in whom I had not the remotest interest. We now had cute sayings and all the endless details of feeding, toilet training and child rearing in general that both of us could share.

My mother reveled in grandmotherhood, whereas I, in becoming a grandmother, once the euphoria had worn off, felt as unsure of myself as a teen-ager on a first date. Charmed as I was by my infant granddaughter, I did not look forward to having her become the focus of whatever life my daughter and I had developed together. There was still so much that was unresolved between us, so many inchoate feelings, so many misperceptions to be cleared up. Was it all to be shoved aside, perhaps forever, while we involved ourselves totally in this new creature? I wonder now whether it was jealousy that was eating away at my pleasure and pride. I'm not sure. I remember thinking that, whatever happened, I would not let my daughter and her husband treat me simply as their child's grandmother. I resolved to avoid this dead end and, whatever the risks, find a place in their lives that would permit us to be fully human with each other.

A lusty and many-faceted human being I know who is also a grandmother often expresses her frustrations with the narrow slot in which she feels her son has placed her. Their communication, she says, is confined to an accounting of his children's activities. She is devoted to her grandchildren but, says she, "I also want to hear about *him*, what he's doing, thinking, reading. We used to talk about all sorts of things—politics, music, books, people. Now it's all been reduced to a catalog of how the children are doing in and out of school. And the only use he and his wife have for me is as a baby sitter."

There is the resentment and the sense of being closed out. But the birth of a grandchild can also be a revelatory experience, which opens up new possibilities for the relationship between parent and child. Film maker Lynne Littmann, who produced a documentary film about mothers and daughters, describes how, after the birth of her son, she felt a sudden flash of sympathy and a new, deeper kind of love for her mother. "When she came to see the baby, I saw her for the first time as a mother. Everyone else approached the baby with outstretched arms. But my mother stood there motionless, her hands clasped tightly behind her back. I realized how terrified she must have been when she held me for the first time, just as I was with my baby. And I now understand my mother as I never did before. She could have had my life—she was cheated of it because of the time she was born. I have no problems leaving my baby while I work, but she couldn't do that without taking on a lot of guilt."

Grandmothers who feel cheated as they see their daughters enjoying the best of both worlds may respond by competing for the grandchild's affections; this is their strategy for securing a place in the family, the family role being the only one life has permitted them.

The Competitive Grandparent

The arrival of a grandchild sets up a new family dynamic with a potential for raising existing levels of parent-child tension, or even for generating hostilities where none existed before. In the three-decker family, the grandchild becomes the most likely pawn in a power struggle between parents and grandparents. In many cases, it's an uneven match, with some important advantages on the grandparents' side.

The parents have the day-to-day responsibilities for the children; they are the disciplinarians, the ones who must say "no" and "don't." As a rule, grandpar-

ents have little or no responsibility for their grandchildren and, even if they wished to discipline them,
feel as if they are in no position to do so. The child
soon catches on and turns to the grandparent for
sympathy and comfort, which the grandparent is
usually ready and eager to provide. And the battle is
joined, with parent and grandparent tossing verbal
grenades at each other. Parent accuses grandparent
of spoiling the child; grandparent retaliates with, "If
anyone's spoiling the child, it's you." Parent says: "I
have a right to raise my children in my own way."
Grandparent: "I raised a couple of children myself
and didn't do so badly." And on and on they go, neither side willing to yield or compromise in this battle
of the generations.

A favorite ploy of competitive grandparents is
using the power of the purse to strengthen their position with the grandchildren. I know a grandmother
with a high-paying administrative position who never
visits her grandchildren without bringing them expensive gifts. Her son and daughter-in-law live in
modest circumstances and feel that Grandma is placing them at a disadvantage. "She's buying the kids'
affection," they say. "And when they ask us for
something we can't afford to get them, they say,
'Never mind, we'll ask Grandma; she'll get it for
us.' "

This same grandmother told me about the time
she sent a check to her son and daughter-in-law so
that they could take the children on a holiday outing:
"My daughter-in-law tore up the check. She won't
take money from me; it offends her pride. She's not
exactly crazy about my buying clothes and other
stuff for the kids. But they're my grandchildren and
it hurts me to see them do without—just because

their parents are jealous of me. I have some rights too, haven't I?"

A Bill of Rights and Wrongs

The question of grandparents' rights has surfaced in recent years as the rising divorce rate has drastically altered generational connections. Dissension in the family invariably places grandparents in a delicate and difficult position. If they act as family arbiter, they usually find themselves in a no-win situation, and when the conflicts erupt into divorce, the problems multiply like mushrooms in a rain forest.

Scenarios like the following are becoming the rule rather than the exception: Your son and his wife are divorced. Custody of the children went to your son's wife, now your ex-daughter-in-law. Your son has visitation rights, and the children are with him every other weekend. Since this is the only time he has with the children, he has hinted rather strongly that he prefers to have them to himself, although, of course, when he has business or social appointments, it is fine for you to baby sit. Your former daughter-in-law is remarried, and her new husband has brought with him the children of his previous marriage, so that your grandchildren have been absorbed into a new family configuration that has stepsiblings in addition to a stepfather. Since you never got on too well with your former daughter-in-law and your son's replacement is decidedly cool toward you, it seems clear that future contacts with your grandchildren are going to be severely restricted. In fact, you feel that your grandchildren are being taken out of your life, that your role as a grandparent is being vetoed by circumstances over which you have no control.

Joint custody, which is rapidly gaining favor in family law, may ameliorate the situation somewhat, although geographical separation makes equal sharing of the children difficult to implement. Whatever the legal arrangements, divorce has a centrifugal effect, thrusting grandparents further and further out of the family orbit. The hostilities that brought about the split have a way of rubbing off on older and younger generations, giving grandparents good reason to worry about their grandchildren being pitted against them.

Feeling that their hold on the grandchildren is precarious at best, grandparents sometimes understandably attempt to affect the outcome of their child's divorce. But this sort of action, according to lawyers specializing in family law, can bring on a host of unwelcome complications, particularly if the grandparents are wealthy. "They may try to blackmail the court on behalf of their own child," says an attorney with a large divorce practice. "They may say, in effect, 'If my son or daughter gets the child, we'll pay for private school or orthodontia,' or whatever seems like the most effective bargaining chip. Divorces are tough enough on everyone without grandparents getting into the act."

But then, is there anything grandparents can do about problems like these? Do grandparents have any rights? The question is being pondered by legal experts, and in England, from which so much of our law has been borrowed, a "granny rights" law was passed not long ago, providing for grandparents' access to their grandchildren. Something like this will probably be appearing on the American scene before long, but the question that still must be faced is: How useful is the law in generational relationships? Realistically, how many grandparents will wave a legal paper in demanding access to their grandchildren when to do so may clash with the wishes of the custodial parent and, possibly, stepparent? Human emotions have never offered a viable area for legislation, and it is doubtful that the feelings of grandparents can be translated into legal rights that can be enforced to the satisfaction of the parties involved. Any rights that grandparents achieve in regard to their grandchildren will emanate from the nature of the three-way relationship.

The Grandparent as Ex-parent

So here you are—youthful, sexy, brimming over with plans and projects, working at a job or a profession or back at school training for a new career, or maybe still trying to decide what you want to be when you "grow up." And suddenly you've been thrust into this new role. You're a grandma or a grandpa. What do you do now? How do you behave? What do the parents of your new grandchild expect of you, if anything?

For a start, let's look at where you—a parent once removed—stand in relation to your grandchild. During the growing years the parents will, of course, be the major shaping force in the child's life, as you were in your children's lives. But there are spaces in that child's life that only you can fill. You can be the family historian, providing continuity, a link with the past, giving sense and coherence to the otherwise disjointed life of so many families today.

Through you, your grandchild becomes part of the living stream of human history, with a strengthened sense of both past and future. You represent tradition and heritage and a set of lasting values that can serve as a counterpoise to the faddish and the ephemeral.

You are also a model of an earlier generation, a living example of how to grow young while growing old. You are a stereotype smasher, replacing worn-out images with those that are real and relevant for today. "My grandmother," said an eleven-year-old, "is a foxy lady. We have a lot of fun together. She's the way I want to be when I'm her age."

You can be many other things: an arbitrator, taste setter, teacher, mentor, support system; a listening ear; a consultant; and even, when required, a baby sitter. Being a grandparent can be one of the most enjoyable, most rewarding experiences of your life. But this can happen only if you have developed a relationship with your children that makes it all possible.

Becoming a grandparent can advance the state of ex-parenthood, placing it on a more solid basis, but it can also retard or even reverse the process of growing toward a new connection. What does it mean to be a "parent once removed"? It means that you have a dual relationship with your grandchildren—attachment and detachment; it means occupying a special place in each other's lives, a warm and intimate place in which there is no room for demands and obligations. "All the fun of parenthood and none of the problems," I've heard several grandparents say. Or, at least, while sharing your children's concerns and anxieties over the problems, you don't attempt to come up with ready-made solutions.

Your relationship with your children places you in an administrative role and leaves the policy making to them. In other words, you go along with what the parents consider best for the children, and when you are left in charge, you carry out their instructions. Suppose you disapprove of the policies? Listen to a grandmother who describes her eight-year-old granddaughter as thoroughly obnoxious: "But I realize it isn't her fault. My son is a doting father, and he has spoiled her so that she is unbearable. All she has to do is say, in a whining tone of voice that drives me up a wall, 'Daddy, I want—' and he stops whatever he is doing to attend to her. And the mother is just as bad. When we're having a conversation, the child constantly interrupts. Instead of telling her to wait until we finish, the conversation is suspended until she's had her say. I keep telling them that if they go on this way, they'll produce a monster, but it's no use."

Here is a grandmother who is still a parent, who wants to control and direct the upbringing of her granddaughter. She sees the parents as instrumental, the means through which her grandchild is to be raised in accordance with her own views. "But they are ruining her," she would insist. Possibly, although children have been known to survive all manner and modes of upbringing and even grow into reasonably successful adults as long as they were sure of their parents' love, and thanks to the counterforce of peers and other social influences. Still the question remains: What do you do when you honestly believe your children are pursuing a harmful course with *their* children?

There are a few options available to you. You can keep your views to yourself and hope for the best. Or you might initiate a discussion at an impersonal level in an objective, nonaccusatory manner. One set of grandparents went about it this way: They invited their children to an extension course in parenting and aired their concern during the discussion period, placing it in an abstract context. This led to a detailed analysis by the instructor and the other participants that, the grandparents believe, was the beginning of a change for the better in their children's behavior as parents.

The one fatal mistake grandparents can make is to manipulate the grandchild in an attempt to gain points with or against their children. The following samples depict the kinds of communication with grandchildren that are to be avoided at all costs:

- You're selfish and inconsiderate—just like your mother.

- Your parents are such busy people; they have no time for me.

- If you don't get better grades in school, you'll turn out like your father, wasting his life in a crummy little job.

- I don't blame you for being so mad at your mother, but never mind, Granny understands and loves you.

As parents once removed, we can be a source of stability as well as continuity, but our place in the family circle will necessarily be located at some distance from the center. That, as it happens, is where good friends of the family can usually be found and where the relationship between family and friends has the best chance to flourish.

10
Once a Child . . .

Time passes, and your children are now living their own lives, either married or not, as parents or childless. Meanwhile, you have been attempting to move beyond parenthood to a new life of your own and a mature relationship with these familiar strangers, these grown-up people who were once your dependent children. Looking down the road, what do you see? The view is probably hazy. There are tantalizing glimpses of freedom as family responsibilities drop off; and over toward the horizon you can discern the faint outline of experiences and adventures never before available to you.

But you may also be looking at other, less appealing views: the middle years shading inexorably into old age; a steady decline in physical power and attractiveness; the inevitability of eventual retirement from job or business or profession, accompanied by a sharp reduction in income; and the looming prospect of loneliness as death claims your elderly parents, your spouse, lifelong friends, colleagues, and other associates while, as a man in his early seventies said, "the world fills up with strangers."

Where do you turn, almost as if by instinct, for comfort and protection against these threatening vistas? To your adult children, of course, who are on the upswing in their personal lives and careers and who will certainly be eager to make some small return to you on your very large investment in them. You begin to rationalize: They are, after all, your flesh and blood; surely you have the right to expect that they will now be concerned about you as you have always been concerned about them.

In this frame of mind, you begin to slide back from ex-parenthood—but not back to the role of parent. This time you are looking for someone to act as parent to you. A process of reversal is taking place, which will be complete, bringing you full circle, when your adult child cooperates by assuming the role of parent to the parent.

Role Reversal

The desire for that warm, uncritical love that we remember receiving from our parents becomes more acute when those parents die and, for the first time in our lives, we are without a generational buffer between us and mortality. Now we begin seeking that lost love from our grown children, encouraging them to slip into the role of parent as we, the parent, revert to the role of child.

Why does the adult child take on the parental role? "It's a way of getting yours back," says a twenty-three-year-old woman whose European-born parents married late and are now in their seventies. "I have a very authoritarian father whose word was law around our house. He's a loving, family-centered man and I'm devoted to him, but I still carry around some of the resentment I felt because of the way he imposed *his* rules and *his* standards on me. There was no appeal from his decisions. I guess that's why I left him as soon as I could—I was only seventeen. And now that Dad is elderly and looks to me for advice and guidance on many things—like finances and problems with my mother, who suffers from depression—well, I've got to admit, I get a certain satisfaction out of telling him what I think he ought to do, laying down the law, you might say. It helps me work out some of the tensions that built up in me over the years."

When role reversal is set in motion, parent and child replay an old drama in which power and responsibility shift from one to the other. As our grown sons and daughters take on the developmental tasks of adulthood, it becomes almost irresistible for them, from their position of newly gained power and status, to assert themselves against us, their no-longer-young parents. When this happens, it is ironic to see how the children repeat the mistakes of their parents. The attempt to impose one's generational value system on another generation, the judgmental approach to the other person's choices and decisions—these behavioral echoes from the past are heard once more, growing louder and clearer as the child steps into the parental role.

An elegantly groomed woman of fifty reflects on her experience in acting as a parent to her eighty-year-old father, who, after the death of his wife, had gone on living alone in the large, rambling house where he had grown up and had raised his children: "I thought it was ridiculous for him to rattle around in that old barn of a place," the daughter says. "It had seven bedrooms, most of which he kept closed off. It cost a small fortune to heat, and it seemed such a lonely way to live. I kept trying to persuade him to sell the house and move into an apartment in a residential community for the elderly, and, finally, I succeeded. Well, it was a terrible mistake and I've always regretted it. He was miserable in the apartment, and I think, for the first time in his life, he was really lonely. All those memories in the old house were company for him. He became ill soon after the move and I had to put him into a nursing home, where he died not long afterward. You can't imagine how many times I've wished I could go back and undo what I did. But at the time it seemed like the sensible thing to do. I took it as my responsibility to look after him according to what I thought best."

There are times when the adult child feels compelled to take on the role of parent to the parent, when there seems no way to avoid it. This happens most frequently in the case of the widowed parent, particularly the mother who has lived a sheltered life in the home and is suddenly left to her own resources, which are likely to be pitifully meager. Her adult children see no alternative but to take over as protector and decision maker, shepherding her through the events and crises of her life.

It's easier, of course, and more comfortable to perpetuate a longstanding relationship by simply switching roles than to change it into something else. But it also means going on with the evasions and pretenses that are used to prop up attachments that have outlived their usefulness. By acting as parent to the parent, the adult child is fostering illusions that can only lead to disillusionment somewhere down the road. As parents in our midyears we are not in need of a surrogate father or mother. What we do need is a solicitous friend who, coming out of a younger generation, can help us keep in touch with a changing world while, at the same time, respecting our right and ability to follow our own path in that world. In this way, we can make contact with each other while retaining our autonomy, with neither parent nor child requiring the other to satisfy emotional cravings that can never be satisfied by another human being.

Adult children who have been successful in establishing this kind of relationship with their parents agree that it grows out of a calculated decision to level with Mom and Dad, even if that means jeopardizing the relationship. I talked with one woman, the mother of a two-year-old, who turned this corner with her mother only after the death of her father. "My father," she began, "was a six-foot-four hulk of a man, a southern gentleman, and my mother grew up on the streets of New York. Their marriage was a keg of dynamite waiting for a lighted match. She just niggled, niggled, niggled away at him, while he struggled to keep himself under control—and at a physical cost none of us understood at the time. There was a sick, dangerous game going on, my mother bringing my father to the edge of violence, then retreating into guilt and self-pity. And we all went along with it; I guess we were afraid of what would happen if there were a confrontation. But only twice in all their years together did he use his physical superiority over her. The first time, my brother and I—I was about sixteen at the time—came home from school and my father said, 'It would be better for your mother if you stayed outside for a few hours. I've bound and gagged her—loosely but enough to keep her quiet—and it would be humiliating for her to let you see her. As soon as she'll talk to me like a human being, I'll untie her.'

"Well, we went outside, thinking it was the best thing he'd ever done, and would you believe it, she convinced him after three hours that she wouldn't make any more scenes, and he had just barely unbound her and taken the gag out of her mouth when she tore outside, yelling loud enough for the whole neighborhood to hear. The next time he used physical force, he had known for two years without telling any of us that he had cancer. She was at him again, rubbing away like sandpaper at all his sore spots, when he suddenly let loose and punched the wall right by her face. It was the first time I'd ever seen my mother looking as if she were going to faint. He said to her, 'I could have killed you a long time ago. From now on, just leave me alone.'

"A few months later he died and, of course, my mother felt guilty as hell. I was living in San Francisco by then, and she moved right nearby. Day after day she did her mea-culpa-poor-little-me number, unloading all of it onto my shoulders. And I let her do it to me, until I began to realize she was using me as she had used my father, as she had used her parents—as an outlet for her bitterness and disappointment. She was making me responsible for her, turning me into her mother; if there was one thing I didn't want, that was it.

"So one day, just as she was starting on her you're-so-good-to-me-I-don't-deserve-it-after-what-I-did-to-your-father routine, I took a chance. I dropped the sympathetic poor-little-you act and said, 'C'mon, cut the bullshit. Did you love him?' Well, that knocked the breath out of her, and when she recovered, she said, 'Of course I loved him.' 'Well, for Chrissake,' I told her, 'hang on to that and let the rest go.'

"That was the beginning of what you might call a new era in our lives. For the first time I began talking to her as if she were a responsible adult. It's taken years, but I'm beginning to see changes. She's found herself a job as a bookkeeper with a social agency—it's the first time she's ever worked at a paying job—and she's become interested in other people's problems, the people who come to the agency. She's made a few friends; she never had any friends before, I guess because she was so self-absorbed no one would put up with her. These days she actually talks about things outside of herself. Sometimes I almost enjoy having a conversation with her. Can you believe it?"

Beginnings, Endings, Continuities

When parents and adult children discover that they enjoy each other as interesting people who are fun to be with, the sensation can be oddly disorienting. It is, understandably, disturbing when people you've known all your life begin revealing facets of which you were never aware. You wonder: Where have I been? Why haven't I noticed? How can people be involved in the closest of all possible relationships and know so little about each other?

The "shock of recognition," in Edmund Wilson's

phrase, usually has stronger reverberations in the child than in the parent. We expect children to change as they grow, even though as parents we may do everything in our power to control and direct the changes. But, for the child, the parent represents a fixed identity. When children, of whatever age, refer to "my mother" or "my father," they are specifying a set of attributes that add up to a static and predictable personality. Despite the findings of recent research into adult development, it is still difficult for many people to accept the fact that personality changes—at times quite drastic ones—can occur throughout the adult years during parenthood, grandparenthood, and even greatgrandparenthood.

Adult children often fail to observe these changes in their parents because they prefer not to observe them. In a world that William James has described as "a buzzin', bloomin' confusion," it is comforting to have some unchanging entities to cling to, to be able to go on thinking of good old, or bad old, Mom or Dad, as the case may be. If one has decided that Mom is vain and scatterbrained, and Dad is selfish and rigid, well then, that's that. How disconcerting to discover at some point that Mom is taking a course in psychology and organizing a discussion group called the Jungian Society. Or that Dad is volunteering his weekend time to escort a group of ghetto children to museums, libraries, and athletic events.

We imprint ourselves upon our children with indelible ink during their growing years, and it is extraordinarily difficult to erase or revise those images later on. Jean-Paul Sartre has shown how the Jew has been created in the minds of others, and, similarly, parents are created in the minds of their children. But here again, parents are co-conspirators. Do we really make an effort to challenge these images, or are we afraid that there is nothing to put in their place? Or that if our children discovered who we really are, came to know us, warts and all, they would cast us out of their lives?

Women in their midyears, whose identities have been derived almost entirely from motherhood, are especially vulnerable to these fears. But men are not exempt. The father who has presented himself to his children all along as tough and macho—which he may have been at one time—is reluctant to reveal himself now as a man troubled with doubts and insecurities, who finds his greatest pleasure in watching ballet and reading poetry.

In a sense we are invisible to our children, since we exist only in their heads as images fastened firmly in place. "We live in an invisible humanity," Maurice Nicoll has said, "a humanity of appearances," and nowhere is this gap between appearance and reality more evident than in the parent-child relationship.

The transition from parent to ex-parent begins when we make ourselves fully visible to our children, so that they can see us not only as we are at any given time, but also as possessing an ever-present potential for adaptation and change. This is not a simple feat to accomplish, and it will not happen overnight. It is a gradual development made up of a series of almost imperceptible changes that grow out of an inner search to discover the person buried within the parent.

Who Was I Before I Became a Parent?

Becoming a parent is such a momentous experience that, for many of us, it makes all other personal events insignificant. We feel that nothing we have ever done or been before can compare with this, and suddenly life seems to be divided into before and after parenthood. As our children grow and consume us with their needs and problems, the before-parenthood period recedes faster and faster from our everyday reality, and there are moments when we find it hard to believe that there was ever a time when we were not somebody's mother or father.

Meanwhile a subtle play of forces is transforming us from someone with a specific persona into a generic entity, the Parent. We are being influenced from all directions to cover up that original persona, until it is hidden from view. As a Parent we are expected to tailor our behavior to fit our new status. We are to mind our manners, watch our language, and Set a Good Example. From this point on, whatever we do or say is being registered on our child's sensitive psyche. This new life that has been placed in our charge has taken priority over much that we may wish to do or be.

The United Front

Of the forces that press us into the parental mold, probably the most pernicious is The United Front, through which we maintain that: United we stand, divided we sow confusion in our children. A parental "we" develops, which is made up of two separate "I's" that have been forged together in an uneasy merger, the dominant "I" asserting itself over the submissive one.

The merger of these two I's results in a strange hybrid, the MaPa, which has two separate heads, bodies, and life experiences, but which functions as one in situations involving the children. The MaPa is also referred to as "my parents," as in "My parents are very conservative"; "My parents don't approve of my friends"; "My parents have never been happy about my marriage"; "My parents think we're too permissive with our kids." Whenever I hear adults referring to their parents in this way, I suspect that they have had the MaPa foisted upon them and are no longer capable of separating the creature into individual entities.

The United Front, it is true, succeeds in giving the children a consistent message, but it is a false consistency and they will not be fooled by it for very long. At some point they will arrive at the conclusion that parents are not to be trusted, that they are not what they appear to be. "I used to think of my mother as an appendage to my father," said a twenty-four-year-old woman. "She always agreed with whatever he said, which used to make me so angry, because sometimes he was grossly unfair and I couldn't understand how she could go along with it. Years later, after he was dead, I found out that inside she almost never agreed with him. She used to choke down her real feelings in order to keep the peace. It must have been torture for her to hold back like that all those years, and it kept us from having a good mother-daughter relationship."

The parental "we" is so obstinate that it often

hangs on even after the parents have been separated by death or divorce. A woman in her fifties who has been divorced for eight years admits that she still has difficulty saying "I" when she is talking with her children. She frequently catches herself saying things like "We think you'd have a better time in London than in Paris," and referring to "our house," "our friends," "our investments."

Learning to say "I" and to speak for yourself with your adult children may take a bit of practice. But as you extricate the "I" from the "we" you'll begin to peel away layers of conformity to parental conventions—all those thoughts and desires suppressed "because of the children"—until you finally reach your preparental self. When this happens, it's a born-again experience. There is that girl-woman or boy-man whom you know so well and yet who seems a thousand light-years away from where you are now. Try to remember: What were his/her aspirations, interests, dreams, pleasures, plans, ideas, impulses? How many of these are still retrievable?

At the university where I design programs for adults and counsel adult students, I see a steady stream of people in their midyears who are attempting to salvage something of themselves that, as they are just becoming aware, has been buried beneath a mountain of parental obligations and responsibilities. As is to be expected, more women go through this experience than men. Many of them are relieved to have motherhood behind them, but they are still looking for something to put in its place.

As they search through the debris of the years for glimpses of their prematernal selves, they dredge up clues like these:

- I used to play the piano—not awfully well, but it gave me a great deal of pleasure. Of course, I gave it up when the children came.

- I have a half-finished novel I was working on when the twins arrived. I wonder if I could go back and finish it now ... or maybe start another one.

- I was crazy about sports, especially tennis. Gave both my rackets to my daughter. Haven't been on a court since the children were little.

- I quit college when I got pregnant. I wanted to get a teaching certificate and teach handicapped children. I wonder if it's too late.

- My interest was politics. The year before my first child was born, I ran for the school board. Didn't make it, but I always wanted to try again. Then we had four children one right after the other, and I sort of gave up.

- I was a professional dancer. I couldn't go back to that now, but there must be something else ...

Retrieving your preparental self does not mean tracing your way back into the past. As that far-off image of who you were before you were a mother or father gradually comes into focus, you will probably discover that some of what was once there is gone forever; to that part of your former self you said goodbye a long time ago. But there are other parts that are still alive in you, though they have been long suppressed. These are the continuities that have been only temporarily interrupted by your submersion in parenthood. And there are also possibilities for new starts, beginnings that may lead to—who knows where?

Shedding the Borrowed Identity

One of the beginnings is the shedding of the borrowed identity that so effectively conceals the person within the parent. But this is easier said than done. There is a certain comfort in drawing upon a source outside ourselves for our self-esteem. We may have fallen short in any number of ways in our own lives: We didn't finish that novel or pass the bar exam, and maybe our marriage has been a failure and our sex life generally a mess. But what the hell, we produced a son who heads up his own electronics business or a daughter who is raising a nice family and also building a law practice. Maybe we haven't done so badly after all.

In fact, what we have done is fall into the trap of the borrowed identity. We have become victim of the "my son the doctor syndrome," a game parents play that goes like this: My child is better than yours and therefore I am better than you. From their toilet training through their choice of colleges and mates, the achievements of the children provide us with a never-ending source of material for the game. And the competition can be fierce and relentless as we score points against each other with this child's straight A's and that one's prowess at the piano or Little League.

The woman who has invested herself in motherhood is, of course, a more assiduous game player than her husband, who has his own achievements in his work to draw upon. Of course, the woman with her own career is also less likely to depend upon her children for ego gratification.

But because women have been so conditioned to taking their sense of self from others, even those who are making it in the business or professional world often ignore their own accomplishments while bragging about those of their children. I attended a meeting of professional women not long ago at which, during the coffee break, one of the participants, an attorney who had just won an important case for a corporate client, was proudly describing her son's achievements in DNA research. When I complimented her on her legal victory, she shrugged, muttered something about it being all just part of the day's work, and went back to reciting her son's scientific triumphs.

A child-centered consumer society, as some social critics have observed, fosters the practice of treating children as possessions. Like the car we drive or the house we live in, the child becomes a testimonial to our upward mobility. A son or daughter who is a success or failure by American middle-class standards must share that success or failure with the parents. We instill in our children a keen awareness of their capacity for inducing pride or shame in their mothers and fathers.

Feeling good about an adult child's accomplishments is one thing. It's the kind of feeling you would have for a good friend, which would express itself verbally as: "You've succeeded in what you set out to do, and I'm happy for you." Borrowing a child's identity and using it as a primary source of self-esteem is something else. In the latter case you're saying: "I'm thrilled about your new job, but just remember, if it weren't for me you wouldn't be where you are today. The credit really belongs to me, and I'm going to see that I get it."

But the catch is that neither self-worth nor self-blame can be appropriated from other people. Whatever a child achieves or fails to achieve belongs to that child alone. As ex-parents we have only our own resources to draw upon for either self-esteem or self-criticism. Assessing and nurturing these resources smooths the way for the return of a borrowed identity to the adult child, who is its rightful owner, and the development of an identity of one's own.

Who Will I Be When I Am No Longer a Parent?

The hidden self that emerges from the parent bears a certain resemblance to a prisoner released from a long confinement who is tempted to return to the familiarity of the cell. Even those who have come through the separation trauma relatively unscarred may be shaken by the realization that a centering force has been removed from their lives. A heady sense of freedom mingles with a feeling of panic. Suddenly it seems urgent to find a new focus. But what? And how? Supposing your preparental interests are no longer relevant to you? You no longer want to be a film star or write a best-selling novel, and pursuing a ball on a tennis court or golf course has lost its attraction for you. Where do you go from there?

For the woman who has been totally absorbed by motherhood, there is often a precipitous plunge into whatever time-filling activities come along. She will take up good works, volunteering for one organization after another, throwing herself into each new project with enthusiasm, and wondering why it all leaves her feeling vaguely dissatisfied and depressed. Or, if she takes a paying job, it will probably be one of the low-level retailing or office-work jobs that seem to be reserved for unskilled women in their midyears. Such daily activities, again, will give her so little satisfaction that she will be drawn as if by magnetism back into the orbit of her adult children's lives.

Fathers, as usual, come off better than mothers at this stage, having always had the world of work to absorb their thoughts and energies. But, as psychologists and counselors are discovering, fathers have their own problems in defining their lives in the postparental stage. The "male menopause" that has been much discussed in recent years is often directly linked to the sense of disorientation that accompanies the shelving of the paternal role. The job that made some sense when there was a growing family to support now seems meaningless. The marital and other personal relationships go stale. The persistent question nags away: Is this all there is?

A man at midlife, as Daniel Levinson notes in *The Seasons of a Man's Life,* is suffering a loss in youthful vitality that affects him as an "insult to his youthful narcissistic pride. Although he is not literally close to death or undergoing severe bodily decline, he typically experiences these changes as a fundamental threat."

This is easily the most volatile and precarious stage in the transition to ex-parenthood, a time when the fragile ego, emerging from its snug parental wrappings, is in need of new accouterments to protect it from the shocks it receives during adaptation and change. It is a time for taking personal inventory, for a systematic evaluation of one's resources as a basis for making decisions about where to go from here. Such a self-analysis should include the following considerations:

Personality: Are you conscientious, irresponsible, cheerful, moody, shy, assertive? What do you consider your weaknesses? Your strengths?

Skills and Abilities: What are your outstanding competencies at this time? How would these be augmented by additional education or training?

Interests: What ideas or activities spark your enthusiasm and imagination?

Values: What ethical and moral standards do you feel strongly committed to?

Environments: What kinds of environments are most comfortable for you? (For example, indoors-outdoors; structured-chaotic; few people-many people, etc.)

People: Describe the kinds of people you prefer to be with socially and in a working relationship. If there are significant differences between the two, what does this tell you about the way you are compartmentalizing your life?

Occupation: What would be your ideal job? What is your present job? What do you feel most qualified to do? Is there a gap between the two? What do you have to do to close the gap?

Time: How would you like to spend your
                  leisure time? How are you spending
                  it now?

Deterrents: What issues, people, or problems are
                  keeping you from what you want to do
                  at this time of your life?

You may wish to supplement this type of self-analysis with professional counseling that can help you sort out your options and point you in a realistic direction. But counseling is most effective when it is grafted onto your own objective appraisal, since the ability to make others understand us grows out of our ability to understand ourselves. Unfortunately, as E. F. Schumacher has observed, "The cultivation of self-knowledge has fallen into virtually total neglect except, that is, where it is the object of active suppression."

For parents, the suppression of self-knowledge is a product of the merging of our identities with those of our children. As we become extensions of each other, we lose the capacity for either self- or mutual understanding. That capacity is restored to us as we discover that there is intelligent and fulfilling life after parenthood, and that if we are willing to accept the risks along with the rewards, ex-parenthood can free us from the constraints of the past and make it possible for us to achieve a better relationship with ourselves and our adult children.

The Risks and Rewards of Ex-parenthood

Emerging as a unique individual from the trappings of parenthood may involve the risk of some changes occurring in your network of relationships. You begin to perceive the people in your life with a new clarity and this often strengthens your attachments, but it may also weaken them. Many human connections are preserved primarily through dishonesty; when the pretenses are removed, the relationships come apart. The reason that is given again and again for the dissolution of so many longstanding marriages is: "Once the children left, there was nothing to keep us together."

Self-deception can also preserve the hollow shell of a parent-child relationship. There are parents who come away from every encounter with their adult children feeling hurt and depressed, yet continue to rationalize the behavior of their child and steadfastly maintain that all is well between them. For many years a colleague of mine kept up this fiction in regard to her married son until, upon reaching ex-parenthood, she admitted, "He is cold, self-centered, and capable of cruelty. I feel sorry for my daughter-in-law, who is an intelligent, loving woman. I can't see how she puts up with him." When the inevitable divorce took place, my colleague reported that she and her son rarely saw each other anymore, but she was developing a "beautiful relationship" with her daughter-in-law. "I feel as though I've lost a son and gained a friend" was her comment.

Having considered the risks, what are the rewards? In shedding a role that we have outgrown, we can move on to higher levels of experience. We can break out of that state of "arrested development" in which we were living one-dimensional lives concentrated on the needs and achievements of others, freeing our energies for our own needs and objectives. We can expand our choices and gain greater control over our lives. We can launch a new career or revitalize an old one that may be going stale. We can become more interesting, more amusing, more loving, more sexually attractive.

While this is happening, our connections with others are also being transformed. If a marriage has become unglued because it was held together only "for the sake of the children," it is now possible to seek new more mutually sustaining attachments. And there are numerous instances of wilting marriages that take on new life when the partners rediscover in their new postparental selves some of their preparental attraction for each other.

But the reward that brings many of us our deepest gratification is our new relationship with our adult children. Often the reluctance to give up the parental role is due to the mistaken belief that there is nothing else to replace it. Once we realize that there is something else, that we can have an attachment that reflects the reality of our changing lives, the reluctance is replaced by a willing acceptance of the new relationship.

Tools and Supports

The evolution toward ex-parenthood will vary according to specific situations, but in summing up as we approach the conclusion of this exploration, we can identify four strategies that are generally applicable and that can serve as tools and supports for this new stage of our lives:

1. *The separate and connected self.* For parents of adult children, an essential task is to separate their identities from those of their

children and develop, through careful and honest self-analysis, a deeper sense of their individual selves. Personal freedom and self-actualization are the base upon which the individual builds a structure of relationships that make up his or her world. As the parent moves toward ex-parenthood, the structure can be enlarged with any number of additions, but it should be founded on the needs and interests of the former parent, not those of the adult child.

2. *Self-revealing communication.* In becoming ex-parents, we must discard certain former habits and ritualized behaviors, particularly the use of language for the purposes of concealment and manipulation. Deceiving small children for their own protection—to guard them from infection or accident, for example—is generally regarded as necessary and is standard parental practice. But continuing this practice into the adult years is a form of paternalism whereby parents set themselves up as having superior wisdom about what is in the best interest of their children. Learning to communicate honestly with adult children begins with self-revelation—the willingness to reveal one's thoughts, feelings, and opinions, even in the face of the children's disapproval. Parents who disclose their authentic selves often report that this makes them more interesting to their children. It also makes them better listeners, since their children are more likely to respond in nonstereotyped ways that go below the surface to

reach the parents at a deeper, more attentive level. The ex-parent should make every effort to become a skilled communicator—first, by becoming adept in using language to reveal rather than conceal; and second, by listening attentively and hearing what is actually being said.

3. *From power to contract.* The transformation from parent to ex-parent resembles, in microcosm, the development of a society from monarchy to democracy over the centuries. When the child is small, the parent is an absolute monarch who enforces obedience, presumably in the best interest of the helpless little subject. The relationship is based on an unequal distribution of power between the parties. As the child approaches maturity, the parent should gradually relax the controls, removing them altogether when the child becomes a self-sustaining adult. From this time on, all claims parent and child have had on each other are dissolved, and they should now deal with each other as free individuals, tied together by voluntary agreements or "contracts." Each party should recognize that we are all, to some extent, products of our time, with our own generational values and biases, and should not attempt to force a set of beliefs or code of behavior upon the other. Disagreements and conflicts should be approached as problem-solving situations to be negotiated in an atmosphere of conciliation and compromise. Feelings of power, guilt,

and obligation have no place in this type of relationship.

4. *The changing family.* The transition to ex-parent does not signal the end of the family unit, but rather a change in the family's shape. Like Proteus, the legendary old man of the sea who could readily change his shape, families today shift and fluctuate, arranging and rearranging themselves as circumstances require. Kinship bonds are no longer the only connecting tissue of the family. There are new definitions of families today, such as: "two or more persons who share resources, share responsibility for decisions, share values and goals, and have commitment to one another over time," or "the climate that one 'comes home to,' a network of sharing and commitments regardless of blood, legal ties, adoption, or marriage." The ex-parent should consider developing this new kind of "family," which might include people from various age groups, connected to each other by purely voluntary bonds.

The transition from parent to friend does not mean that the relationship becomes less warm and loving than before. There are instances, of course, as in the case of the woman who "lost a son and gained a friend," in which we find that we and our adult children have grown so far apart that there is nothing left with which to bridge the distance. But, for most of us, the new connection will be closer and deeper than ever before, and the feelings of warmth and affectionate concern will flow between us naturally, without being forced.

As with many other adaptations that we make in the course of our lives, the first one is usually the most difficult. Many ex-parents would agree, I am sure, that after they have found their way to post-parenthood with the first child, it goes more easily and smoothly with subsequent children. This was certainly so for me and my younger daughter; for us, the shift from parent to friend seems to have occurred with almost a complete absence of trauma.

As for my first child, the daughter who shared with me the risks as well as the rewards of our slow, painful evolving toward where we are today, she has, perhaps, said it all in these few lines from one of her letters:

> With each day
> With each growing
> I learn what it is
> To be a woman
> And I grow closer and closer
> To you